The
Lost Kingdom

by

CHESTER BRYANT

illustrated by

MARGARET AYER

THE JUNIOR LITERARY GUILD AND
JULIAN MESSNER, INC.   NEW YORK

‡‡‡‡‡‡‡‡‡‡‡‡ The Lost Kingdom

RODMIKA WAS THIRTEEN years old and compared with most Hindu boys he was big for his age. He lay flat upon the rock, his chin resting on the back of his crossed hands. The sun burned into his bare brown back, and a slight breeze fluttered the loose end of the turban bound about his head. Below him the surface of the pool was ruffled too, hiding for a moment the long, gray shape of Ajgar, the python, that lay on the bottom.

The boy closed his eyes as if it helped him enjoy all the more the cooling movement of the air in the steamy Indian jungle. With the breeze came the fragrance of flowers blooming on a distant hillside.

Rodmika smiled. "The wind is like the great mother of the jungle passing by with flowers in her hair," he said to himself. "The hem of her cotton *sari* drags the pool as she comes, and her sleeve caresses my back. She drifts beyond the pool, gently rustling the leaves high in the forest trees. Now she is only a murmur far away."

He opened his eyes. The pool was still again, but Ajgar had moved. Then a short distance away ripples suddenly circled outward from where the great serpent's head broke the surface.

Its seven-yard-long body trailed like a thick vine into the depths. An innocent teak leaf floating on the water would look the same, thought Rodmika.

The flat head glistened in the sunlight, and Rodmika spoke aloud, "Hear me, O creature without any ears." He laughed and his laughter echoed from the forest beyond the pool, but Ajgar showed no sign of hearing. Reaching cautiously with one hand, the boy grasped a small stone and tapped it sharply against the rock. Again the ripples circled outward from the serpent's head, and like a hand bent at the wrist it rose a few inches out of the water.

Its forked black tongue lapped the air. Rodmika was still again. "Find me, O serpent who listens with his stomach," whispered the boy, teasingly. "Find where the tapping came from that reached thee through the water." The black tongue continued to flash out from between the long closed jaws. Rodmika chuckled. "O one with eyes that never close, see me here upon the rock. As long as I am still, my brown face and the white cotton *puggaree* bound about my head are a part of the rock to thee."

At that moment an excited chattering broke from the tree-tops behind and above him, as the leader of a troop of gray langurs spied the searching head of the python. Then a panic-stricken retreat of the entire tribe of gray monkeys began. Their flight carried them over the narrow end of the pool, as they leaped from tree to tree. Rodmika turned his head to one side and watched. He saw a dozen or more of the four-handed crea-tures in the air at once. Half of them seemed to drop into the leafy branches of one out-stretched limb. It swung down with the sudden weight, and snapped. The scampering gray monkeys caught new branches, but the shock of the broken fall dislodged one baby from where it clung beneath its mother's body, and Rodmika saw it drop like a plummet into the water.

Ajgar saw it too, and felt the impulse of the small body striking the pool come to him through the water. The great serpent lowered its head and began to swim cautiously.

Quickly Rodmika measured the distance from the python to the gray shape struggling helplessly below him. Pushing his turban from his head as he jumped to his feet, he made a low running dive from the rock.

He thought of the python's powerful jaws and long, needle-sharp teeth as he came up a yard short of the baby monkey. Two overhand strokes, and he ducked his head and felt the little hands grasp his thick black hair. He swam on as fast as he could toward a log that sloped into the water. It seemed that he would never reach it. But now his down-surging hand struck it. He struggled to his feet and splashed onto the dry, mossy upper end.

Above the wild screaming of the langurs there was a loud hiss of the serpent at Rodmika's back. The boy whirled and waved his arms, but already Ajgar, puzzled and startled at seeing a man creature where he expected to see only a small monkey, was lashing back upon his own whipping coils to disappear in a burst of foam and spray.

Rodmika sank to the log to get his breath and pulled the little animal from his head. For a moment he held it by its hind legs and shook it. No water came from its nose or mouth. "Thou art all right, little fellow," he said, "thy lungs are dry."

Back on the rock he recovered his turban and dried the little langur with it, then laid it upon the sun-heated stone and covered it against the chill of a new breeze.

The monkeys chattered anxiously, but the wild panic in their hearts was gone. Rodmika was no stranger to them. The mother of the little one crept to the edge of the rock.

"Not yet," cautioned the boy, "let him rest and get warm." He removed his wet *dhoti* from about his waist and spread it on the rock to dry, while he continued his conversation with the mother langur. "Thou *bandar log* must learn that the python thou canst see is harmless. It is the one lying still and unseen upon a shadowy rock that is dangerous." He was careful not to smile at the monkey, for smiling revealed his teeth, and a show of teeth to wild animals, he knew, was taken as a sign of unfriendliness.

Soon the little monkey began to squirm beneath the cotton covering, and presently a small hand found its way out, then its head and shoulders. It sat up, examining the cotton cloth, as the mother approached, chattering nervously. She extended her paw to her baby, but the little one was in no hurry to leave the new-found comfort of Rodmika's *puggaree*. It screamed at its mother and pulled the cloth folds over its tiny man-like face.

The old monkey seemed puzzled for a moment, then impatiently snatched the cloth away and picked up her angry infant. She held it as a human mother holds her child, and as she leaped away to the trees a little head peeped over her shoul-

4

der taking a last look at the boy and his wonderful cotton coverings.

For a few minutes more Rodmika lay on the rock. When his *dhoti* was dry he arose, draped it about his small waist, and squinted at the sun. It was nearing mid-afternoon. For two days he had been in the jungle and his bag of cooked rice was exhausted. He stretched and yawned and turned toward the home of his parents at the American Foundation near the village of Valdapur.

In going from island to island in the watery jungle he was forced twice to swim, but the remainder of the crossings he was able to make either upon logs or through the trees. The way through trees was the hardest and often dangerous. As dangerous, he thought, as swimming through the darkly stained water where crocodiles and pythons lurked.

He was almost two hours reaching the edge of the great swamp, and as he walked along a log he heard the distant jingle of bells. He stopped a moment to listen. The bronze tinkling grew louder as it came to him from the jungle-hidden hillside above.

Rodmika smiled and spoke aloud, as if addressing the small yellow bird that searched industriously through the tangle of vines over-head. "The bells of Swanji, the Dak-runner," he said. "He must have a very important letter for someone." The smile lingered on his face as he remembered how he had often watched the jungle letter carrier jog doggedly along the forest trail with his official pack of letters and the bronze bells strapped about his waist. Then when he would come into view of the American Foundation Buildings, Swanji would break into a full run that set his bells to echoing through the jungle as they were doing now. "Yes," said the boy to himself, "he must have an important letter for someone or he wouldn't be running so hard a full mile from the Foundation."

The bells slowly passed beyond hearing without any slackening of cadence. "He is still running," said Rodmika, and a curious desire to be at home began to well up in his breast. Although Swanji had never in his life brought him a letter and he could think of no reason why he should get one now, he felt a certain uneasiness about it. What if the Dak-runner did have a letter for him, an important letter, and he was not there to receive it. He ran anxiously along the log, dropped to the stony ground and climbed to the foot-path on the hill-side.

The sun was low in the west when Rodmika came over the crest of the hill and looked down the trail toward the big arched sign above the compound gate. Everything was painted red by the setting sun. Still he could read the big letters. "The American Foundation for Famine Relief. Established 1912," it said in English, then beneath it the same thing was said again in Hindi. Rodmika knew the story of the "Foundation," as everyone in the district called it. His father had told him first, then he had heard it over and over in the Foundation school. There had been only one bad famine since the Foundation was established, and it might have been worse had their granaries not been full. Now the Foundation not only stored grain against bad years, but improved seed, sent a surveyor about the country to help level fields for irrigation, and taught better

7

farming methods. It had been a happier land since the coming of the Foundation, so the old ones said. Beyond the Foundation buildings and fields lay the sleepy village of Valdapur, nestled among great banyan trees. Through the green foliage rose the blue smoke of cooking fires and from the branches flapped giant flying foxes on their way to the fruit orchards of the Foundation and the mango trees of the jungle.

Rodmika sauntered down to the gate and looked in. Mr. Towers, the elderly superintendent, and his wife were sitting on a bench built around the trunk of a banyan tree. Squatting near them, sipping a cup of tea, was the letter carrier. Mr. Towers held a paper in his hand, reading aloud from it, as Mrs. Towers examined it over his shoulder.

Rodmika felt a thin wave of disappointment sweep over him; then he shrugged his small shoulders and sat down in the shade of a bush near the open gate. He hadn't really expected a letter, he told himself, so why should he feel disappointed at getting none?

Unwinding his turban, he wiped the perspiration from his face with it and held out the long thin cloth so that the evening breeze billowed it out like a banner. The flowing garment caught Mr. Towers' eye. He put down the paper quickly and called, "Rodmika! Go to the fields and bring your father. We have some news for him. It's about his land."

Rodmika was up and away like an antelope, his disappointment lost in a sudden surge of elation. His feeling about the letter had been almost right after all. What could be more important to him than news about his father's land?

He went first to the kaffir field. There he found the men and women coming away with their baskets and bags loaded with the rich grain heads.

"Thy father, Jankari, has left us and gone to the threshing floor," said one of the workers in reply to his question. "He was told that the boys tending the bullocks there were idling. Boys had better follow thee to the jungle than try threshing rice alone." There was more, but Rodmika didn't stay to hear it. He left the foot-path and ran through the grove of coconut palms.

As he ran he thought of the land that had been possessed by his grandfather and their grandfathers before them. Then, long ago, in the years of the famine his father's father had left the land and had taken his family to the Foundation. Rodmika's father had been brought up at the Foundation, and he, Rodmika, had been born there.

The bullocks and the boys had been sent away when Rodmika reached the threshing floor, but his father was there winnowing the grains from the chaff in the light wind.

"Father!" he cried breathlessly. "Come to the office quickly. Mr. Towers has news about our land."

Jankari put down his three cornered winnowing basket. A slow light came into his eyes. "Can it be, at last?" he said.

"Hurry, Father," urged the boy.

Jankari carefully covered the mound of grain with a square of canvas before he left the threshing floor, but when he walked he showed his eagerness to get the news. Rodmika had to run to keep up with him.

9

"Well, Jankari," said Mr. Towers, extending his hand, as they entered the compound, "you are to be congratulated. I have a letter here which states that you are now a landholder. All question concerning your ownership of your father's old farm and the ancient stone house has been cleared up."

Rodmika watched a smile spread over his father's face. "Thank you, Sir," said Jankari in his clear English. "I know that if it had not been for you and Mrs. Towers we would never have got our land back."

"All we did," put in Mrs. Towers, "was to tell them about the cobra mark on your chest."

Jankari self-consciously touched the dull blue crown of the seven-headed cobra which his father had made with the needled device upon his skin. And Rodmika touched the similar mark upon his own chest. "It has always been like that, Sir. Every father in my family before me since time beyond memory has placed that mark upon his oldest son."

"That did it," said Mr. Towers. He laughed and ran his fingers through his thick gray hair. "I thought it was a heathenish thing to do when I saw your father put that mark on you, and also when you put it on Rodmika. But now I can see that it has served a good practical purpose."

"When will you be leaving us?" asked Mrs. Towers.

Jankari hesitated a moment, then answered, "I would like to go soon, but I will wait until the harvest is complete. I know a good farmer who will come to take my place and manage the workers."

"Then have him come at once," said Mr. Towers. "You will

need all the time you can get to prepare your land for the next monsoon."

"I remember a small stream that ran through the farm from the hills," said Jankari. "I hope to use it to water my fields as we do here. Perhaps I can make a crop of grain before the monsoon."

"All the more reason why you should be off soon," said Mr. Towers.

* * *

In the days that followed, Rodmika had no time to revisit the great swamp that lay between the mission and the deeper, darker morass of Hara Daldal. He worked hard, loading the bullock cart with furniture, tools, and implements.

On the night before their departure he lay upon his *charpoy* beneath the stars listening to the familiar sounds about him. His younger brother, Dobarra, lay beside him, sleepily asking questions. His father sat in the doorway, and inside the small bungalow by the light of the *maum butti,* the flickering wick lamp, his mother sang softly to his baby sister.

"I will miss the swamp and the animals and birds there," said Rodmika idly.

"You will miss the swamp, yes," said his father, "but how would you like to have instead Hara Daldal, the great green jungle, sunken land that is green even now when most of the trees of the forest have lost their leaves?"

Rodmika sat up. "Hara Daldal?"

"None other," said his father, "and almost at your door."

"But," said the boy, puzzled, "how can it be, when the great sunken jungle is just beyond our own swamp, while our new home is a nine-day journey from here?"

The father chuckled. "True enough. Beyond our swamp is the great morass of Hara Daldal and beyond that our new home. It is only some twenty miles across, the *sahibs* say, but no man could make his way through it. A long journey, as you shall see."

The boy smiled dreamily as he lay back. "I love the jungle," he said. "I love the dark waters, the high trees, the dense thickets. I like to lie on a limb and watch Bhalu the bear rip open a bee tree and stick his head into the comb. He snorts and blows as he sucks out the honey. Then the bees get to his eyes and nose and Bhalu runs in blind circles, fighting and grunting, until he plunges into the water. Sometimes when he goes away and the bees become quiet there is some honey left for me."

Dobarra giggled in delight, and the father spoke to him. "Thy brother is a strange one, little son. The jungle is more his home than a house. The birds, the deer, even Dukkra, the wild boar, seem to know him."

"And the monkeys," added Dobarra, eagerly. "Both the red monkeys and the gray monkeys with the black cheeks speak to him as if he were their brother. But to me they only chatter and show their teeth."

It was decided that Rodmika was to accompany his father on the first trip to the new home and return later with the bullock cart for the family and the remainder of their possessions. On the following morning they departed with the cart stacked high and with Boda, their gentle, but ponderous, water buffalo following on a lead rope.

For nine days and nights they were on the road. At sunset of the last day they drew up at the ruins of a heavy-walled stone house overgrown with vines and choked by a jungle thicket that had crept in during the long years of desertion.

"This is our home," said Jankari. "And see, the palms are alive and the little stream beyond the house still runs."

Rodmika climbed down and looked at the molding stone blocks that made up the walls, and at the gaping shutterless windows. "It has no roof," he called back, "but the stone work is sound. It doesn't look like the home of a farmer, with those rich carvings about the windows."

"Yes," said his father, "I remember it from my childhood. Every stranger who came here said it seemed more like the palace of a Rajah than the home of a jungle farmer."

At that moment there was the chirping of many small birds and the low whirr of their wings. The boy and the man looked up as cloud after cloud of winged things swept over. "I remember that, too," said Jankari. "In the evening they fly to the hills and in the morning they return for some strange reason to Hara Daldal. It is just one more mystery that the dark sunken land holds."

They worked their way to an open window of the house and climbed through. "Our grandfathers built well," observed Rodmika. "It took many men and many bullocks to set these heavy stones in place."

He climbed gingerly over fallen teak beams and the broken

13

tiles, deep in dust and laced with a matting of vines. The tiles clanked and snapped under his weight. Suddenly in a flurry of dust a shadowy shape in dark fur fled silently over the wreckage and disappeared through the doorway.

"What was that?" asked Jankari.

"I hardly saw it," replied Rodmika, "but I think it was a mongoose. If it was, that means good luck to this house."

"Yes," said his father, "they say a mongoose is a good sign and there is reason for it too, for a mongoose will keep the snakes away."

Rodmika was looking cautiously through the growing dusk into a dark corner of the room.

"What do you see?" asked his father.

"Something moved," he replied. A low growl greeted Rodmika's advance.

"Careful, son," warned Jankari.

"I see it now," said the boy. "It's a young mongoose. It is backed into a corner."

"Mind those teeth," said Jankari. "A mongoose can be very vicious."

Rodmika laughed softly as he bent down. The growling continued for a little while, then subsided. "It is a baby one," he said presently. "That growling was only bluff, like the blowing of the rat snake." He stood up cuddling the tiny ferret-like animal in his hands. "Now it trembles, but soon it will be used to me. I will make a pet of it for Dobarra."

His father smiled at him in the twilight. "When you are too busy to go to the jungle, you bring the jungle to you."

14

They climbed back through the window and returned to the bullock cart. While Jankari prepared a cooking fire, Rodmika arranged a basket to hold the mongoose. Then he milked Boda and poured some of the milk into a small dish. At first the little animal seemed uninterested in it.

"I'll change that," said Rodmika eagerly.

He touched a finger to the milk, then touched the drop of white liquid which remained on it to the nose of the mongoose. It licked the drop away, squeaked hungrily and licked the boy's finger. But the finger moved, and the little red tongue followed until the finger was again touching the milk in the dish. Now it was lapping with the dainty noise of a hungry kitten. The boy and his father chuckled as they watched it.

"There is something else I want you to see," said Jankari. "Take the lantern and go to the doorway. See what is carved in the stone above it."

Rodmika took the lantern and Jankari watched him go through the tangle to the doorway of the old house. He stood before it a moment with the lantern upraised, then returned to the cooking fire.

"The cobra crown," he said, with wonder in his voice. "It is carved there. The very mark which we bear upon our chests."

"The same," said his father, "and so lost in forgotten time that no one knows or may ever know the why of it."

They were silent for a while. The rice on the fire began to boil, and the air was filled with the spicy aroma of curry.

"This is a good homecoming," said Rodmika.

"Yes," said his father. "This is a good homecoming."

OR TEN DAYS the sun rose and set in a cloudless sky, as Rodmika and his father worked at repairing the house and cleaning out the big stone-curbed well. They replaced the heavy teak timbers above the walls and reclaimed the unbroken tiles for the roof. When they had done all that they could, the doors and window shutters hung on new hinges, the flagstones of the floors were reset, and the roof was covered except for a space near the ridgepole.

Jankari stood with his son in the center of the larger room looking up through the naked rafters at the sky. "Hinges, nails, and other such things made of metal, are what use up our money," said the father, shaking into his hand the few coins that remained in the leather bag tied to his sash. "Still we must go to the village and buy tiles to finish the roof."

"We could make them," suggested Rodmika. "We have good red earth, and hard teak firewood."

"It would take time," said Jankari with a sigh, "and time is costly. We are farmers and our time belongs to the soil."

"Then let us thatch the hole in the roof," said Rodmika cheerfully. "That's what most farmers do for their entire roofs. There are long fronds hanging from our palms that I could pull down and weave together."

The father nodded his head thoughtfully. "We may have to do that," he said, "until our harvest is in. My time must be spent in the fields. There is a dam to be built, and there are water ditches to be dug. Then I must take Boda and begin clearing brush from the field. There is so much to be done, and soon you must return to the Foundation for your mother and little brother and sister. Yes, it would be wise to thatch the hole in the roof, and that job I will leave to thee."

As Rodmika climbed the towering palms, he got his first view of the country that surrounded his new home. In all directions there was jungle. To the South rose the high forest-clad hills through which they had traveled in coming to their new home. To the East hung the dust of Kumba village, six miles away on the river. Beyond the low near-by hills Rodmika looked into the shimmering heat of the great swamps and tangled forests of Hara Daldal stretching away northward and westward into the ever-hanging mists. A gentle breeze rattled the fronds about him and brought to him the damp heavy fragrance of the sunken jungle. The boy breathed it deeply and gazed longingly toward the lost land lying beyond the curtain of rising vapors.

"They say it is evil," he whispered. "Abandoned, the *sahibs* say. Not even the forest guards go there. But I shall go there." As he worked, he glanced again and again toward Hara Daldal. Occasionally his father's shout came to him from the field, and Boda's grunt as she leaned into her yoke to drag away the brush.

On the trail to Kumba new dust floated in the treetops. And as Rodmika pulled the loose fronds from the last of the palms he saw, with a start, the cause of it. Riding a pony from the thicket came a bearded man with a long-barreled gun across his saddle before him.

The boy flattened himself against the swaying trunk of the palm and tried to swallow the excited pounding of his heart. His father shouted again at Boda and the bearded one stopped his pony to listen. Slowly he shifted his gun and dismounted, then, leading the shaggy little animal, he disappeared in the direction of the field.

Rodmika slipped silently to the ground, ran across the compound, and plunged into the jungle that separated the house from the field. Fear grew in his throat as he ran. Briers clawed at him, and vines tripped him. The jungle which had always been his friend seemed to turn against him, determined to keep him from reaching his father in time to warn him. A low limb snatched his turban from his head, and a monkey screeched at him from the treetops.

A moment later he tumbled wildly through the brush fence into the field. There was still time. His father labored alone with the big buffalo not a hundred yards away. Rodmika ran to him gasping for breath.

Jankari saw the excitement and fear in his eyes and placed his hands upon his son's shoulders to steady him. "My son," he said in their native speech, "hast a black snake bitten thee?"

"Nay, Father," panted Rodmika, "a man comes."

"A man comes," repeated Jankari. "Is that something to make thee lose thy head and crash like a bull elephant through the jungle? Thy face is scratched in a dozen places."

"But a man comes from the village. A man with a beard and a gun. A red beard and a long, shiny gun. He comes through the jungle." Rodmika swung his finger, pointing toward the thicket. There was still no one in sight.

A slow smile came over Jankari's face. "My son is too much in the jungle," he said. "He can read the signs of animals, but not those of man. By the red beard, the one who comes is a Hajiwalla, a Muslim who has made the pilgrimage of his religion to Mecca. As a true Muslim he dislikes Dukkra, the wild boar, which men of his sect call unclean. So, he gets a pig license and a gun. He hunts Dukkra and drives him and his brood deep into the jungle. That is good for us, too, for in one night a drove of wild pigs can ruin a grain field. This man who comes is our friend, as you shall soon see."

Rodmika was too exhausted to speak. He kept his eyes uneasily upon the gap in the brush fence, and presently saw the bearded man lead his pony through it into the field. As he approached, the boy saw that their visitor was old, and that his face seemed to wrinkle in a perpetual smile. He lifted the hand that held the pony's reins and greeted them with the word that is the same in all of India's many languages, "Salaam."

"Salaam," they replied in return.

"I am Abdul," said the old man, "and I am called the pig hunter." He spoke in Hindustani, his own language, but both Rodmika and his father understood it and spoke it well. When they answered, they also spoke in Hindustani.

"I am Jankari, the owner of this farm," said the father. "This is my son, Rodmika."

The old man squinted his eyes and leaned close to Jankari. Jankari chuckled and wiped the red field dust from his bare chest. "Ah, there it is," said Abdul, "the crown of the seven-headed cobra. Thou art the rightful one."

Rodmika wiped his chest, though no dust hid the mark on him. Abdul patted him on the shoulder, and said, "And thou art a true son. I knew the old ones here long ago before the years of famine. I bid thee welcome. If pigs bother thy crops, send for me. If a tiger or leopard threatens thy cattle, leave word in the village and I will come. I go all over this land searching for these evil-doers."

"Dost thou go into Hara Daldal?" asked Rodmika timidly.

"Nay, baba." The old hunter laughed. "No man goes into that vile place. It is full of darkness and evil."

"He has spent his life near the Green Jungle," said Jankari, "but on the other side at the Farm Foundation of the American *sahibs*. There he could not go far into the jungle because of too much water."

"Here there is much water, too," put in Abdul, "but one who understands the jungle could find a way into its depths. Still, it is not for me, and for no one else that I have known. Not even the officer *sahibs* of the reserved forests go there."

"My son must think of schooling, not jungles," said Jankari. "Is there a schoolmaster in the village?"

"There is one wise enough to be a schoolmaster," replied Abdul. "He would take a bright scholar, I think. He is even older than I, and speaks the English of the *sahibs*. His name is Vallabiah, and he lives in a little house near the *miadan,* where he keeps records of some sort."

"I will visit him soon," said Jankari. "Perhaps by the time my son brings his mother and the small children from the Foundation to their new home, it will be arranged."

* * *

Three days later Rodmika began the long trip back to the Foundation. Since the cart was loaded lightly with only a sack of grain for the bullocks and a bag of rice for himself, he completed the nine day journey in less than seven days.

He had little time at the Foundation to visit with his young friends. Every minute of the day was spent in finding places in the cart for the many things his mother wanted to take to their new home. Then there were gifts from Mrs. Towers, and at the last minute strings of marigolds placed about their necks by their Indian friends and neighbors.

As the cart lumbered past the open gates of the office compound, Mr. and Mrs. Towers came out to bid them farewell. The boy's mother, always timid in the presence of those outside her family, lowered her unsmiling eyes to the child she held in her arms.

"You are leaving at the wrong time, Rodmika," said Mr. Towers. "My grandson is coming out to India next monsoon to spend a year with us. He is about your age. You two could have some fine times in the jungle."

"And we are getting a new surveyor, too," added Mrs. Towers. "He will be here soon. He could teach you high school subjects." She stepped closer to the cart and placed her hand on the mother's arm. "Jolanda," she said, "this is a wonderful thing. You mustn't feel bad about leaving."

"Yes, Madam," replied the mother without looking up.

"We will come back for a visit someday," promised Rodmika.

"Rodmika will find a way through the jungle," said Dobarra shyly in hesitant English.

Mrs. Towers smiled and Mr. Towers winked at Rodmika. "Your little brother is giving you a big order, Rodmika."

"I have wondered, Sir," said Rodmika thoughtfully, "why a road hasn't been built through Green Jungle to Kumba village on the other side. Kumba is the principal village of the district.

22

Still to reach it from the farms here we must travel nine days over rough jungle trails and pass through two other states."

Mr. Towers pushed back his *topee* and scratched his head. "I am afraid you don't know what that would take. To build a road through Green Jungle would mean building an earthen embankment about twenty miles long. Nobody knows how deep the water is in the middle of that jungle. No one has ever been there. On the older maps it was noted as unadministered territory, and, in fact, it is still unadministered. You can rest assured that if there was any dry land in Green Jungle it would have been discovered long ago."

"Still," said Rodmika, "I'll try to find a way."

"I like to hear you talk like that," said Mrs. Towers. "India, with its new independence, is going to need men who won't be discouraged. You keep trying. It would be a big help to us in our work of teaching better farming methods if we had a direct road to Kumba."

"Don't be too discouraged about the road, Rodmika," added Mr. Towers. "If we can't have a new one across the middle of Green Jungle we will have the next best thing. We are urging the government to build a bridge across the lower end where the old Wardlo ferry was before the roads washed out. That will save three days' time in traveling from here to Kumba by bullock cart. Our new surveyor is going to work with the Public Works Department engineers on the survey."

"But that will still be too far to walk," said Rodmika.

"Yes, it will," agreed Mrs. Towers. "You look for a crossing. Who knows, you may be able to find a way across by boat."

"Here, the sun is getting high," said Mr. Towers suddenly. "We are keeping these people from their journey." He touched his wife's arm and they stepped back from the cart. "Good luck to you, and don't forget to give your bullocks a rest at noon. You'll travel faster that way."

As the cart wound its way up the hill toward the forest road, Rodmika looked back under the big hood of woven palm fronds that covered the cart. His mother was settling herself and the children among the bags and bedclothes for the long trip. Often she turned her face toward the small white-washed house where they had lived for so many years. Finally it was no longer in sight, and the boy saw her pull the end of her *sari,* which was draped about her head, down over her eyes and lower her head into her hands. Tears filled his own eyes at the sight of his mother's weeping.

He turned back to the road and put the bullocks into a trot as they passed over the crest of the hill. A moment later he felt Dobarra's small hand upon his shoulder, and a damp nose and a tearful little face against his.

"We are leaving our home," sobbed the child. "Mother says that we children were born there, and that no other place will be the same."

"We are going to a new and better home," said Rodmika, bravely. He spoke aloud so that his mother could hear above the clatter of the heavy wheels over the stony ground. "We are going to a new home that is all our own. The red soil will be our own. The stone house will be our own, the house where our father was born and his father before him. They were happy there. We will be happy too. We will forget that there was ever another place we called home."

The small arm circled tighter about Rodmika's neck. "Dost thou promise it?" asked Dobarra.

"I promise it," replied Rodmika.

Three

ENEATH THE STARRY heavens the Indian jungle lay resting, but awake. Like a sleepless old man tossing under his blanket, life in the forest-covered hills and valleys was never still. The dim light of a lantern shone on the winding jungle road, making the boughs of the massive trees interlaced above it seem like giant fingers clasped in meditation.

To Rodmika, sitting on the tongue of the cart, the road seemed a dull tunnel, slowly and miraculously opening a few yards before the yoked bullocks and closing quickly behind the cart. Swinging from the axle beneath the cart, the smoky lantern cast strange walking shadows of the thick wheel-spokes upon the tangle of undergrowth on either side. But stranger still were the shadows cast by the lumbering bullocks, striding like monsters into the forest beyond.

The road dipped slightly to let a small stream gurgle and sparkle across. Rodmika stopped the weary animals so that they might drink. With the last echo of the clacking wheel hubs he heard the faraway cry of a jackal and the distant call of a leopard. Behind him under the high cart hood came the regular breathing of Dobarra and his mother. His baby sister, nestling in the mother's arms, seemed to make no sound at all. They had been asleep for several hours and Rodmika hoped that they would not awaken until they reached their new home. The jungle that lay between the last village and the farm was forbidding even in daylight. They might become frightened if they woke up to see that they were no longer on the wide high-road over which they had traveled for more than a week.

When the bullocks had finished drinking, the boy spoke to them, and they pulled the heavy cart through the stream and on along the road. Ahead of them at the next turning a great silvery shape stood in their path, staring blankly toward the swaying lantern. Its black eyes threw back the light as two dully glowing coals of fire, and from its proud head spread lofty antlers that glistened as though they were covered with frost.

Rodmika smiled and spoke in a low voice, more to himself than to the jungle creature. "It is I, O Sambar. It is I who spreads salt upon the log by the pool for thy kind to lick."

The great Sambar stamped one foot and snorted loudly, then like the crash of a falling tree dashed out of the light into the forest.

The boy chuckled softly; he was happy. In a few more hours they would all be together with their father. Something touched his neck, and he quickly looked around.

"Why dost thou laugh?" asked Dobarra in a low whisper.

"Sleep, little monkey," Rodmika replied. "I shall awaken thee when we reach the hill that looks down upon our new home. It will be light enough to see then."

"What caused thee to laugh into the night?" insisted the younger boy.

"I was thinking of how happy mother will be in our new home when she sees how comfortable Father has made it."

"Will it not be like it was at the Foundation? Will there not be school and children?"

"It will be different," said Rodmika. "There will be no children, and little school for us until we find a way to cross Hara Daldal to the Foundation."

"And thou will soon find a way across," said Dobarra with assurance.

The soft laughter that rose from Rodmika's throat died suddenly. Dobarra grasped his shoulder with one hand while he pointed along the cart track with the other.

"What is that?" the small boy asked in an uncertain voice.

A lean-bodied creature that had been lying in the grass between the wheel ruts got to its feet and stretched like a house cat after a nap. Then it looked curiously toward the oncoming cart.

Before answering, Rodmika braced his bare feet against the cart tongue and wrapped the line fastened to the bullocks' nose rings more securely about his hand. "It is a leopard," he whispered hoarsely. "But don't be afraid. There will be no danger unless the bullocks become frightened."

Dobarra put both arms about his brother's neck and with his face against his brother's said, "That creature has no spots. Does the leopard have no spots?"

"It is a leopard, and it has spots," explained Rodmika. "But in this dim light the spots are lost, and it looks gray. A tiger, too, would look gray and without stripes in this light."

"Art thou certain that this is no tiger?" asked Dobarra. "They are both cats."

"This one is a leopard—panther, the *sahibs* call it," answered Rodmika. "Its body is thinner than a tiger's, its head smaller; and it has a longer tail. There it is leaving the road. It will lie in the ditch and watch us pass."

The glowing eyes, like quiet fires, peered through the brush as they passed. The bullocks, catching the scent where the cat had lain, snorted and dashed wildly ahead, tossing their long painted horns. But Rodmika was ready, and his skillful handling of the line kept them to the road and they soon settled into their normal pace. The baby became fretful, but after a few soothing words from the mother it was quiet again.

"Father says that thou knowest the jungle better than he," commented Dobarra, slowly releasing his hold on his brother's neck. "He said that we would be safe with thee anywhere in the jungle."

"Then sleep, *baba*," said Rodmika, "and be fresh when day comes and we reach our farm. I have tamed a mongoose for thee to play with, and there is a mouse deer in rocks of a nearby hillside which would like to be a friend."

With a sleepy sigh Dobarra lay back among the bags of clothes which served as his bed, and soon his regular breathing told that he slept.

Rodmika rose from his uncomfortable seat and looked anxiously back through the high arched hood at the road. He was not happy at what he saw. Just as he had thought, the leopard was following the cart. It ran along the wheel track until it was within leaping distance, then stopped, caution overcoming its curiosity. It dropped to the ground and waited. Impatiently it moved the end of its long tail slowly from side to side. The cart drew away from it as it watched.

The boy stepped back into the cart, taking care not to dis-

turb his family, and examined the laced netting of *coir* rope which he had woven over the back end opening. It seemed strong enough, but to make sure he added more rope to it.

Again the leopard ran toward the cart and this time came closer and gave a short bounding leap. Then it lost its nerve and stopped again. Rodmika's heart pounded in his throat. Streams of sweat trickled down his face. It was plain that the savage jungle cat was gradually overcoming its fear of the dimly glowing lantern. And to make matters worse, in spite of its poor sense of smell, it had probably caught the scent of the six chickens which were in a coop tied to the back of the cart.

Rodmika returned to his place on the shaft and urged the bullocks on at a faster pace. A moment later his mother called softly to him.

"Yes, Mother," he answered, turning back to her.

"Dost thou see the two great cats that follow us?" she asked uneasily.

Two great cats! thought Rodmika in alarm. He stood up and

stared back on the trail. It was true. Another and larger leopard had joined the first in its game of stalking the cart. Aloud he answered, "Yes, Mother, I see them. Day will come soon and they will grow tired of following and go back to their lair."

Thus assured, the woman lay down again. A shiver ran

through Rodmika's youthful frame as he watched the spotted beasts. They stayed closer now; each seemed jealous lest the other get closer to the cart than he. As soon as one lay down the other ran ahead of it. Sometimes they struck playfully at each other in passing.

They were becoming harder to see now, and with a sudden frightening thought Rodmika knew why. The oil in the lantern was burning out. Soon there would be complete darkness. He looked longingly toward the east, but the starlight that filtered through the tangle of limbs showed no dawn paleness. His mother and little brother breathed peacefully. They trusted him to get them safely home. He wanted to awaken them so that they might share his fear, but after a moment the panicky feeling passed. They could do nothing and would only become terrified. It was up to him alone to keep the leopards at a safe distance from the cart.

The feeble flame in the lantern made one last fluttering struggle and went out. Black darkness shut down over the cart. Rodmika could hear the swish of the grass as the leopards made their short quick charges through it. Sooner or later, he feared, one of them would find the courage to leap upon the cart. He considered cutting the chicken coop loose. In it were five fine, white leghorn hens and a rooster that Mrs. Towers had given his mother. He decided against it, but still, he thought, it would be better to lose the chickens than have the cats spring upon the cart.

There was another lamp packed among their things. He didn't know where to find it, but cautiously thrusting his arm here and there among their possessions he began to search. All he found was their provisions. Disgusted, he drew his hand away smeared with buffalo butter.

An angry snarl came to him from just beyond one wheel. The bullock on that side snorted in fear and veered away. The other wheel went into the ditch. Rodmika hauled hard on the line to bring the cart back onto the road just in time to prevent it from overturning.

He knew he could wait no longer. There was a small box of matches among the provisions, and he reached for it. Only four were left. He struck one. As it flared up he let it drop to a wheel track. It went out as soon as it touched the ground. Then he tore a piece of cloth from his turban and lighted it. It burned dully, and Rodmika was about to abandon it when a small bright flame burst from the cloth where butter from his fingers had soaked in. Without wasting another moment he reached for more butter, smeared it upon the burning cloth, and dropped the cloth to the road.

His breath quickening, Rodmika turned and watched the flame as the cart passed beyond it. The big cats stopped, but not for long. As soon as the flame died down he heard them rushing through the grass again. The next piece of cloth he soaked more thoroughly with butter, but in attempting to light it broke the match and dropped it.

His hand trembled as he reached for the last match. Carefully he scratched it on the side of the box and applied it to the butter-soaked cloth. Again the flame in the road stopped the leopards.

The trail turned and Rodmika put the weary grunting bullocks into a fast trot, but the trip had been hard, and they soon slowed to a walk. Neither the boy's bamboo goad nor the terrifying scent of the spotted cats could force them on any faster.

Anxiously Rodmika watched the back trail. As the cart rounded another turn, the bounding gray shapes came into view—they were racing for the cart. Then from the slope below the road came a screaming cry: "Moo-oor, moo-oor!" The cats heard it too and stopped in their tracks. It was the waking call of a peafowl. It screamed again, and to it was added the shrill challenge of a jungle cock.

The leopards followed the cart a little farther, but kept looking toward the thicket. Suddenly they leaped into the undergrowth and vanished. It was not until then that the boy realized that with all its tropical suddenness day had come. The forest became thinner, and soon the cart came out onto a rocky hillside.

Before them lay the low hills of dry brown forests and stretching away into the concealing haze like a sea of green was Hara Daldal. The rising sun played warmly on the tiles and thatch of a house nestled with its small fields and clusters of date and coconut palms and fig trees among the hills.

"Wake up, *baba*," called Rodmika, shaking Dobarra's shoulder. "We're almost home."

Both the small boy and his mother sat up and blinked in the sunlight. Rodmika pointed to the red field in the distance where a man held a plow drawn by a ponderous water buffalo.

34

"There is father!" exclaimed Dobarra. "It must be. He is plowing with Boda."

"Yes," agreed Rodmika, "it is father."

As the cart rumbled down the hill, their father looked toward them and waved. Then, unfastening the buffalo, he led her toward the house to await their arrival.

When the bullocks trotted into the compound a half hour later Jankari came out to greet them and announce that the morning meal was ready. While he helped the family to the ground, Rodmika propped up the tongue of the cart and led the bullocks from their yoke.

"Didst thou have any adventures on the way?" the father asked Dobarra.

"We saw a leopard," replied the boy, "but it ran away. I was frightened, but Rodmika wasn't. He is brave."

"Yes," added the mother, smiling at her older son, "Rodmika is brave. I know because, although I lay still, I did not sleep. I saw all that happened during the night."

Jankari laid one hand tenderly upon her shoulder. "Thou art still weary with fear. I can see it in thine eyes. Thou must learn that in the affairs of the jungle our son is no longer a child. My family was in safe hands."

Four

ODMIKA OPENED HIS eyes and looked out through the open window at the faint stars twinkling in a pale sky. The white rooster crowed within the bamboo coop where it and the hens were shut in for the night. The aroma of frying rice cakes, mixed with charcoal smoke came to the boy's nostrils. He stretched and sat up.

For a full minute he could not remember why he was to get up so early. Three weeks had passed since he had brought his mother and the small children from the Foundation. The house and farm had begun to feel like home to them now. Rodmika had worked hard with his father in the fields, but he had found time to visit the outer edges of Hara Daldal. He had discovered it to be denser, darker, and more difficult to get through than any jungle he had been in. It called to him more strongly than ever before. Then there were the squared stones he had stumbled upon out in the wild, sunken tangle. At the thought of the stones he remembered why the whole household was stirring so early.

"It is the day the *pundit* Vallabiah comes from the village," Rodmika whispered. He quickly dressed himself in a fresh *dhoti* and went out to the well to draw water.

Vallabiah was to be his teacher. He had had no lessons yet, but they were to begin soon. Jankari had arranged for the boy to walk to the village one day a week to be taught more about weights and measures and the value of figures. But today it was going to be different. Today Vallabiah was coming to visit him, and not about lessons.

He recalled the evening his father returned from the village to say to his wife, "Our friend, the wise *pundit* of Kumba, will come here to speak with our son. I offered to send the lad to him, for the man is too old to travel these rough trails even in a light *bundy*. But, no, he will not have it. He must see our son here."

"Perhaps," ventured the mother, "he would see if our son will make a good scholar."

"No, no," protested Jankari. "It has something to do with Hara Daldal. I told him that our son was too much with the jungle. It is not good for one so young to spend one night after another in that dark, evil place, then come home with a look in his eyes as if a faraway call still rang in his ears. It was when I told of the squared stones Rodmika had found that the old one said that he would come here."

After the morning meal Rodmika completed his appointed tasks quickly and trotted up the trail toward Kumba to meet his mentor. The first rays of the sun were making diamonds of the dew drops and pearl nets of spider webs when he heard the rumble of the steel-tired *bundy* over the stony ground. He climbed upon a rock beside the road to wait.

Through the still, bare branches he first caught the bobbing of a gray pony's head, the flash of a blue turban, then a red one. The pony walked slowly. In the morning silence he heard voices carrying clearly through the trees. The blue turban spoke in disgust and the red turban replied in age and patience.

"It is no affair of mine," said the owner of the blue turban who held the pony's reins, "but why should one of thy wisdom travel six hard miles to talk to a jungle boy?"

From the white beard beneath the red turban came a chuckle and an answer. "Perhaps I shall gain more wisdom thereby. Perhaps I shall gain what I seek. Many have sought it before me. They have all failed. Perhaps they were too haughty to talk with a jungle boy."

"Thou art worse than a white *sahib*," said the driver, "and heaven knows that they are all mad. I was in the camp of the forest conservator for a number of days once. He is the superior to my superior. He has wealth and great power. He holds my life in his hands, all the villagers from here to the sea bow down when he passes. But he is as mad as a hyena in hot weather.

"We came to river with our tongues hanging out for thirst, but would the great white *sahib* drink? No. He bade me dip up a pot of water which he made very hot over his primus stove. Then, he sat fanning it to make it cool, all the while his tongue growing so thick he could hardly swallow. Only when it was cool again would he drink. Now, O Father, would you believe me, he reviled me and called me a junglie-one because that night I lighted a *butti* at my head to keep away evil spirits."

So interested had Rodmika become in the driver's recitation that he let the cart pass him before he moved. But the driver and the old man saw him at once. "Hold there!" cried the driver, pulling the pony to a stop. "How far is it to the farm of the jungle dwellers, little brother?"

Before the boy could answer, the old man spoke through the white beard that hid the lower part of his face as effectively as the turban hid the upper part. "Art thou the son of the farmer who lives in the house of ancient stone?"

Rodmika was fascinated. Only the old man's long hooked

nose and bright sparkling eyes were visible between the beard and the turban.

"Speak, child, where are thy manners?" barked the driver. "The sage of Kumba questions thee."

"I am the one thou seekest, O Father," replied Rodmika in confusion, "and I have come along the road to lead thee to my father's house."

The driver chuckled and tugged at his gray mustache. "The way is clear," he said. "The pony could follow it unguided. Climb up beside me and learn how a *bundy* breaks the bones of one who comes over this rough road to visit thee."

Rodmika climbed up and sat on the foot-board beside the driver.

"It can't be seen that I am a forest guard," volunteered the driver, "since I left my brass buckle and number at the village. But a forest guard I am, and Gugu Dall is my name. Thou shall hear of me often when there is a forest blaze or there are logs to be counted."

"I know by thy blue *puggaree* and blue shirt that thou art a forest guard," said Rodmika timidly.

"And by thy wagging tongue, Gugu Dall, I know thee for a forest guard," said the old man with a deep laugh. "Let that be a warning to thee, little brother. He who spends his days and nights alone in the forest grows a tongue as long as a lash and as loose as a mountain stream."

Gugu Dall roared with laughter and slapped his naked thigh with his big hand. Then to the pony he shouted, "Get on with thee before I lash thy hide with something other than the sound of my ill-bred tongue." They all laughed, and the pony put back his ears and broke into a trot which he kept up until they reached the house where Jankari stood at the well-curb to welcome them.

While Jankari drew water for the pony and talked with the forest guard, Rodmika followed Vallabiah as he walked about the compound, examining the house and the stones in the wall that partially surrounded it. Finally he sat upon a bench beneath a clump of papaya trees and turned his attention to the boy.

"I am told that you speak English," said the old man in English.

"Yes," said Rodmika in the same tongue. "We spoke English at the Foundation."

"And you speak the vernaculars of the district as well, I suppose?"

"Most of them," replied Rodmika.

Vallabiah studied the boy a moment and spoke again. "How far have you gone into the great green jungle?"

"Not far, Sir," replied Rodmika. "There is so much water, and in many places the trees are too far apart for me to climb through the branches from one island to the next."

The old man slowly shook his head, which in India is an agreeable sign. "Yes, that is true," he said, "but as the dry season advances, the water will go down a little. Just before the monsoon rains begin in June you will find much of it gone in the edges of the jungle."

Rodmika looked at his visitor with new interest. In spite of the great red turban he could see his aged face more clearly. His eyes sparkled intensely beneath his shaggy white eyebrows.

41

They were searching eyes, but still they were friendly. The long hooked nose had a searching appearance, too. Old Vallabiah, thought Rodmika, like Abdul, is also a hunter, though he uses no gun. "Do you search for something in the jungle, Sir?" he asked.

The old eyes continued to sparkle and a long lean finger moved out to touch the dull blue mark of the cobra crown upon the boy's chest. Then he waved toward the same design carved above the door. "I search for thee, *baba*," he said in the vernacular which was more softly spoken than English. He hesitated a moment and chuckled at the look of amazement on Rodmika's face.

"Now, my lad," he said resuming his English speech, "tell me about the squared stones which you found in the sunken land of green jungle. Those stones may tell us much."

"The first I saw from a tree," Rodmika began. "I was about three miles from here and about a mile and a half into the jungle itself. I could go no further. Below me was black water, but clear enough to see that it was no deeper than half my height. I saw on the bottom what at first seemed to be a box twice the span of my hand, square at each end and half as long as my arm. There were no crocodiles near, so I climbed down. As soon as I touched it I knew that it was not a box but a stone. It was heavy and moved slowly, but I got it into my arms and carried it to a small island. I scraped the moss from it to see if it had some inscription on it but it had none."

"Did you hold the stone above water as you took it to the island?" asked the old man with an amused twinkle in his eyes.

"Yes, Sir," answered the boy.

"Then you made extra work for yourself," said Vallabiah. "If you had not lifted the stone above the surface of the water, the water would have helped hold it up."

"Water hold up a stone?" asked Rodmika.

"Yes, it helps. All heavy things become lighter in water, even iron and stone. The reason is this, water has weight also, and it presses upward against any object submerged in it with a force equal to the weight of the water which the object occupies."

Rodmika smiled. "Do you mean that if a portion of water the size of the stone weighs ten pounds that the stone in water would weigh ten pounds less than it does in air?"

"Exactly," said Vallabiah. "That is known as the principle of Archimedes and someday I shall tell you how that old Greek discovered it long ago."

"Is this the way you teach your scholars, Sir?" asked Rodmika with a grin.

The old man wagged his head. "That was your first lesson. The whole world is your schoolroom. Knowledge is found in everything. My duty is to act as a guide and point the facts out to you until your own eyes can see them. Now let us get back to the stones you found."

Vallabiah bent down and examined the paving stones of the compound, then rose stiffly and walked to the stone wall. "Were all the stones you found exactly alike?"

"I found two, Sir, and they were exactly alike."

"And they were like these, too, were they not?" asked the old man, swinging his hand around to indicate the stones of the wall and the pavement.

"Exactly, sir," replied Rodmika, a puzzled expression growing on his face. "But why would someone take stones from our compound and drop them far out into Hara Daldal?"

Vallabiah returned to his seat beneath the papaya trees. "Those stones were not taken from this compound," he said. "Such stones are found in houses and walls throughout this part of India. No one knows where they came from, except that they were paving stones laid in some ancient king's highway. See how the edges were worn round on one side but they remain sharp on the other. Those worn sides formed the surface of the highway. The wheels of carts, feet of men, the hooves of bullocks, donkeys, and horses, and the pads of camels rounded those stones on their upper sides.

"Perhaps two thousand years ago it was a flourishing highway. We know that it existed, but not in the oldest legends of this district is it mentioned. Nowhere in known history is it written."

Rodmika looked up from the pavement with wonder in his eyes. "The ones in our pavement are rounded on the upper side, Sir. Does that mean that this compound was a part of the old highway?"

"I believe it does," answered Vallabiah. "And your father's house was a station for the ancient kings' officers—perhaps custom officers, but we can't be sure. Not until you find some undisturbed portion of that pavement to tell us more."

"Perhaps when the land sank, the kingdom was destroyed," ventured Rodmika. "And the highway was not used any more."

"And," added Vallabiah, "people took away the paving

stones to build houses and walls. They couldn't take these because one very powerful had possession of this house. They
took what they could from the jungle, but they could go only
so far. Beyond that point the pavement still remains."

A strange yearning began to grow in Rodmika's heart. He
stared hard at the stones as if he expected them to give up their
secret. Slowly he looked up at the old man. "Why, O Father,"
he asked softly in his native tongue, "dost thou search for me?"
He touched the cobra mark upon his chest. "Thou seest wonders in these squared things, while I see only stones. Tell me
how I can see these wonders. Tell me the why of it all, O
Father."

Old Vallabiah looked pleased. "Men may ask what, or how,
or where, but only a true scholar asks why. I can tell thee that
there was once a road of smooth stone. Thou, by finding the
stones in the jungle, hast told me where it went. This knowledge I sought for many years. Thou hast given it to me in a
moment. Now I return it to thee ten-fold. Go into the jungle
and seek thyself, little brother. Seek the meaning of the mark
upon thy chest. I cannot tell thee the why of it all. That is for
thee alone to find."

* * *

Many weeks were to pass before Rodmika could go into the
unknown depths of the jungle, but the old teacher's words had
burned deeply into his mind. Working in the field, doing prob-
lems on his slate the words rang in his ears, "Go into the jungle
and seek thyself, little brother. Seek the meaning of the mark
on thy chest."

45

T WAS LIKE any other warm sunny morning of India in wintertime that Rodmika, with his hoe upon his shoulder, went singing through the forest. High in the foliage of a mango tree a green parrot scolded at him and a gray langur grinned from a boulder. Further along a tiny mouse-deer, no bigger than a cat, crept from the dense brush of a rocky hillside and let the boy stroke its back.

When he continued on his way the little animal followed him. "Here," Rodmika called to the mouse-deer, "you go back into the brush. I am going to an open field to work. This is no place for a *pesura*. A great eagle would certainly sweep down and carry thee off." The small creature paid no attention to the warning, but when they had reached the end of the rocky hillside it turned of its own accord and disappeared into the undergrowth.

The needs of the new grain field demanded all of Rodmika's time now, and he was compelled to put out of his mind, for a while, all thought of a trip deep into Hara Daldal. On reaching the field he went industriously to work on the watering ditches. He had been there about an hour when he heard something moving beyond the brush fence in the jungle. Thinking that it

46

was, perhaps, Cheetal, the spotted deer and his family, he didn't look up until he was ready for a short rest.

Then what he saw sent a quiver of fear tingling up his back. Standing in the edge of the jungle was Abdul, the pig hunter, but no kindly smile broke through his red beard as he saluted his young friend in the field.

The heavy hammers of the old hunter's double-barreled rifle were lowered upon gleaming new copper caps. The weapon was ready for instant use.

"Welcome, O Abdul," greeted the boy when he could find his voice. He went to the Muslim's side. "You will find no pigs here. Dukkra, the wild boar has taken his tribe to the hills." In spite of his bold words Rodmika's fear grew heavier. He knew that Abdul was not seeking wild pigs.

"I am looking for a brave man," said the old hunter. And now the twinkle shone briefly in his bright brown eyes. "Dost thou think I might find one in this field?"

"Then it must be true," said Rodmika in a hushed voice, "that Bagh, the destroying tiger has come to our jungle."

"Yes, *baba,*" confirmed Abdul. "I have trailed him for five days, and last night he killed a jungle man's calf near the river. He dragged it into a *nulla* and ate his fill. Bagh now lies sleeping in the thicket on yonder hillside."

"A brave man thou seekest, Abdul, but here is only a trembling boy. Wait and I shall bring my father."

"There is no time for that, *baba.* Bagh sleeps deeply during the morning hours. He must be found before he begins to roll and toss in the mid-day heat. Rodmika, I know, does not want

47

the animals of his jungle destroyed by this great evil tiger. Is that not so, *baba?*" Old Abdul chuckled and shifted his rifle to the crook of his other arm.

"Lead on, O Abdul," said Rodmika, dropping his hoe. "I will help thee find this tiger. But what can I do? I have no rifle, no knife, no spear, not even a well-balanced club."

Abdul swung around and strode off toward the hillside. "The *baba* has eyes sharper than those of the eagle," he said, and his voice showed that he was pleased at the boy's courage. "And ears," he continued, "that catch sounds that even the spotted deer would miss. But, best of all, he understands the language of the jungle. The *baba* has all these, while poor old Abdul has only his rifle."

They both laughed. Of course Abdul was old, and his ears and eyes were not as good as they once had been. Rodmika knew that, but he also knew that age had in no way decreased his friend's wisdom. Abdul was still more than a match for any marauding tiger. His courage rose with the thought.

"Speak on, Abdul," he begged. "Tell me how my eyes and ears can help rid the jungle of Bagh?"

"First," instructed the hunter, "tell me all that the many creatures of the jungle tell thee. Some I shall hear also, but many sounds will be too faint for my old ears. The crows will be the loudest and the freest with their advice, but they are seldom wise and often are entirely false. It is the *bandar log*, the monkey people, who are our true sentries. Does the *baba* understand their warnings?"

"The *bandar log* are almost always within hearing, and they see all things. I have not heard them speak of Bagh but if they think him a greater evil than Ajgar, the python, then we will surely hear much of their very worst language on the hillside near the tiger."

"And what do the monkey people say of thee, little brother?" asked Abdul.

"The ones that know me only blink and scratch when I pass, but the grandfather of a new tribe will look at me, puff out his cheeks, and say in a loud hollow voice, 'Hoo!' which is like saying to his family, 'No danger, my children, but look at the funny creature all covered with cloth that walks on his hind hands beneath us.' "

"Enough. We must speak only above the lowest whisper," cautioned Abdul as they reached the foot of the hill, "for we are nearing the thicket where the tiger lies asleep."

After going a short distance farther they came to a *nulla* with a flat sandy bottom. The old hunter pointed to deep footprints in the sand. "There, see his *pug* marks," he said. He lowered his rifle to the sand and knelt beside the tracks. Gently with the tip of a finger he touched the edge of one impression in the sand. "See, *baba,* these tracks are only a few hours old. The sand is still soft and particles of it fall into the track at the slightest touch."

Rodmika dropped down beside him and touched the tracks as Abdul had done. "They are not the same shape," the boy observed. "One is the hind foot and the other is the front."

"And which is which, *baba?*" asked Abdul, as if he were a teacher testing the knowledge of a pupil.

Rodmika studied the footprints a moment, then pointed, "That is the hind foot. The pad is wider. The pad of the front foot is longer but not so wide."

"And is this evil creature a male tiger or a female one?" Abdul asked again.

"The sand is firm," answered Rodmika, "but the tracks are deep. And they are large. This one must be a great male."

"That is right," said Abdul. "There is another sign, too. The foot pad is rounder in the male and the toe pads are also rounder. In the female all cushions, or pads, are longer. Didst the *baba* know that?"

"*Nay,* Abdul," said Rodmika, "I did not, but I shall not forget it."

They rose to their feet and continued silently up the hill. A few minutes later Abdul lifted one hand in a signal to stop, and they strained their ears against the faint sounds of the jungle. "What dost thou hear?" whispered Abdul.

"I hear the monkeys far away. And somewhere in the distance the sweet singing *bul-bul,* but now its song has changed to scolding."

"I, too, hear the monkeys," said Abdul. "They are beyond the crest of the hill. There the jungle is dense and many large trees have low out-spread limbs. Baba will climb among those limbs and spy ahead for me. He will be safe above the ground."

"But," protested Rodmika, swallowing hard, "I have never prowled after a tiger before. When I see one in the jungle I am not afraid for I am about my business and he is about his. This is different. He will know that I am stalking him. The tiger has great claws and long white teeth, and he, too, can climb trees."

Abdul smiled through his red beard. "Have no fear of that," he whispered reassuringly. "Bagh will look no higher than his shoulders, unless *baba* makes a noise. Man is all that he fears, and man, he thinks, walks only upon the ground."

51

"And wilt thou be in a tree also, Abdul?" asked Rodmika.

"Nay, baba, I must remain on the ground where I can swing my rifle with freedom."

Rodmika shivered at the thought of Abdul's facing an angry tiger on foot. Slowly they advanced up the hillside, with Abdul stopping now and then to point out a broken twig or the grass bent down where the beast had stepped in going to his hiding place. Finally they reached the big trees at the top of the hill. At the hunter's signal Rodmika climbed among the low limbs and moved ahead toward the chattering monkeys. Yes, he felt safer now.

He studied every inch of ground that lay between him and the next tree before going forward and motioning Abdul to follow. Most of the time he had to return to the ground and creep to the next tree, but occasionally he managed to climb through the limbs from one to another.

The monkey noises halted suddenly, then a gray leader gave a hollow "Hoo," which told Rodmika that they had seen him and, perhaps, were welcoming him in shouting insults at their common enemy, the tiger. He moved with greater caution now and studied the brush with added thoroughness before motioning Abdul to come on.

At last he was directly beneath a group of monkeys that kept to the tops of the highest trees. They seemed to peer into a small *miadan*-like opening in the jungle straight ahead. Rodmika was forced to move into the trees on the edge of the opening before he could study it clearly.

It was about a hundred feet across and covered with dry grass except where two jack-fruit trees grew close together in the center. A few bolder monkeys were in the tops of the jack-fruit trees, and they were looking straight down into the dense brush that grew between them.

Rodmika pondered for a moment the wisdom of attempting to cross through the grass, and decided against it. Instead he returned to Abdul to report what he had found.

"I know the place well," recalled the hunter. "I once shot a leopard there that had killed a charcoal burner's goat. Go around the clearing. You will find a banyan tree with limbs that reach out to those in the center. Remember I watch thee every moment. Point to Old Stripes as soon as thou hast seen him, and follow every one of his moves with thy pointing finger until thou hast heard the roar of my rifle."

"If thou miss?" sighed Rodmika uneasily.

"In that case I still have another loaded barrel. But I shall try not to miss with the first one." Abdul sounded confident. "Go, thou," he instructed, "and be careful to make no noise, for when Bagh's sleep is disturbed he may become angry and try to kill anything in his path."

"Why don't the *bandar log* awaken him with their screeching and chattering?" asked the boy.

"He is used to their noise," replied Abdul impatiently. "It means nothing to him. Now, go."

Rodmika, slowly and with careful deliberation, worked his way into the jack-fruit trees. Soon he was poised above the dense undergrowth between them. He peered through the dark shadows below him, but his eyes revealed nothing that looked like a tiger.

Suddenly a sound in the dry leaves at the outer edge of the clearing drew his attention. There among the surrounding trees stood Cheetal, the spotted deer, his antlers glistening in the sunlight. Behind him were a doe and a small fawn. He had seen them many times in the forest before and they seemed almost as tame as his father's bullocks.

"Go back," cried Rodmika silently in his mind. "Run as thou has never run before!"

The stag flicked the flies away with a quick movement of one ear then the other. As he glanced up at the noisy langurs, the wrinkles above his big black eyes seemed to give him a puzzled expression. He stomped one pointed hoof and whirled as if about to dash back into the jungle. Then, looking over his shoulder, he saw Rodmika on the limb. The puzzled look left his eyes. Fear and suspicion left him. The stag turned again and led its family into the clearing to feed.

Rodmika's heart ached. The deer were walking directly into a deadly trap, and all because they had seen him. Closer and closer they moved toward the jack-fruit trees.

A stick snapped. Rodmika looked down. A shadow moved. Then a long tawny body, whose stripes had blended so well with the grass and branches became suddenly visible as it began to move. The great beast lowered its surly head and crept toward the deer family, not twenty feet away.

The boy pointed at the tiger. His finger swung slowly as the big cat moved. Abdul would know that Bagh was awake and stirring. At the edge of the brush the tiger stopped and crouched to spring upon the deer.

54

Rodmika searched his mind for something he might do to save them. He might shout, but no, Abdul, too, was in danger. He must do nothing that would make the old hunter's problem harder. He must do nothing but point at the tiger with his finger. It was such a little thing, but, still, it was the duty Abdul had given him. It was the one and only thing he could do to guide the hunter.

The tiger's muscles hardened and the end of its tail moved slowly from side to side. Cheetal walked peacefully toward it. Rodmika bit his lip. His pointing finger trembled.

Then, like a suddenly released arrow, the striped cat shot forward over the brush. The mighty roar in its throat was lost in the greater roar of Abdul's rifle. Startled, the deer ran to the edge of the clearing, turned about and stomped his foot, while the monkeys in one screaming mass made off through the tree-tops. Acrid blue smoke and the smell of cordite drifted to Rodmika's nostrils. Nothing moved in the brush. The tiger lay still.

"*Baba,*" called Abdul softly.

"Yes, O great and brave hunter," answered Rodmika, trembling with joyful excitement.

"Does the striped one move? He has fallen where my eyes do not reach."

"Come, O Abdul. Bagh lies as still as stone. The jungle dwellers can thank thee, Abdul."

"They can thank thee also, little brother," said the hunter advancing cautiously. "Without thy aid I would have failed. I could not see the tiger to shoot it until it was in the air, but I was ready. I had the *baba's* pointing finger to guide me."

WEEK LATER ON Vallabiah's second visit to the little farm in the jungle he told Rodmika the meaning of the flocks of birds which they saw almost daily swarming like smoke clouds from the depths of Hara Daldal. In the late afternoon they walked along the trail that led to the crest of a hill overlooking the first dark waters of the great morass.

"When I was young," said the old teacher, "I too had the interest you show in this dark mysterious land that lies before us, but I did not have your knowledge of it. I went many times to the watery edge but darkness and wild animals always turned me back. Wild animals, ugh!" the old man seemed to shudder at the mention of them. "I don't know why India must be cursed with so many. My interest is in forgotten people and the ruins of their dwellings, but see now, where other races of men lived long ago, wild animals of the most vicious sort live today. I leave it all to you, my lad. To search out India's lost past, as well as your own, one must love and understand wild animals as well as the history of the past."

"I love the animals," replied Rodmika, "but as for the history of the past, where shall I find it?"

Old Vallabiah closed his eyes and thrust out his lower lip as he thought for a moment. "The house in which you live could give you some splendid history of what you seek."

"How, Sir?"

"Consider this," the old man went on. "Though it is made of stone it is not a stone structure. That tells us how old it is. We have learned that about two thousand years ago Indians began to use stone to build imitation wooden temples and palaces. They quarried their building stone in long heavy pieces to resemble squared teak logs. Some they cut to show the bark.

"To span the top of a doorway or a window they used a massive stone lintel. They did not learn until much later, when invaders came in from the northwest, that a true stone structure was made of small stones; that an archway made of small, especially shaped stones was much stronger than even the heaviest lintel. Even when the Buddhists of that age carved their cave temples in the living rock they made the rock resemble wood."

A twittering flock of birds swept over the trees in noisy undulating flight. "They have begun," said Vallabiah. "It was these flocks that gave me my first hope of finding my way into the jungle. It reminded me of the time I lived with an uncle near the river Ganges. There were great *Jheels* surrounding our village, vast marshes covered with tall grasses and reeds. During the day flocks of birds of every conceivable kind, it seemed, swarmed over the *Jheels* to feed."

"Then," exclaimed Rodmika, "there must be a grassland somewhere in Green Jungle."

"There assuredly is," said the old man. His eyes sparkled as he seemed to recall an almost forgotten adventure. "I went

57

to it. I was certain there was such a place when I saw the birds. I reasoned that perhaps the going would be easier in a grass jungle. It would have been had we not encountered the awful monster of the grasslands, Gonda."

"Gonda," repeated Rodmika. "I have never heard of Gonda."

"Nor had I. And I have never encountered him since, I am glad to say. I might never have known what it was, so slight is my knowledge of animals, had I not told a man from Assam about it. Gonda, he said it was, but he was reluctant to believe that such a creature lived outside his own northern *terai*."

"But you did see it here in Hara Daldal?" asked Rodmika excitedly.

"Not only did I see it," said the old man, "but I felt the thrust of its heavy hairless shoulder as it knocked me to the ground. Then it dashed on to toss Beg Mohammed high into the air. Beg Mohammed with the gun of his grandfather was my companion. Had he not shot at the beast we might not have been attacked, but he had to prove himself a hunter. Luckily the monster charged on, shaking the earth and blowing like a bull elephant gone mad. When I recovered my senses, I went to my groaning friend. He was hurt, but even more frightened. We went back to our bamboo raft and spent the next three days getting home. We forgot the gun, and poor Beg Mohammed was forced to work five years to pay his grandfather for it."

Rodmika laughed with Vallabiah at the memory, and for a moment afterward he was silent. "Sir," he said presently, "must I, too, make a raft in order to reach the grasslands?"

"That is for you to decide. The raft was the invention of two village youths who feared the jungle and could think of no better way to travel through it."

A dark swarm of birds came over them and blotted out the evening sky. The whirr of their wings drowned out their words. Vallabiah motioned toward a tall tree, and Rodmika ran to it and began to climb.

From among the upper branches he scanned the dark blue-green roof of the far-stretching jungle, and like a sailor taking his bearings, the boy reasoned that with the lowering sun in his eyes and the birds flying toward him by the right hand, he would seek the grassland by traveling in a northwesterly direction. When he returned to the ground he asked, "Is the grassland northwest of us?"

"I cannot say," replied Vallabiah. "I trust your knowledge of the jungle will lead you there. It may be toward this grassland that the pavement goes. Somewhere in the jungle it ends and there long ago was a mighty city of a mighty kingdom. In this lost kingdom, wherever it may be, you will surely find the secret of the seven-headed cobra."

* * *

Two nights later Jankari announced that the grain field would require no more attention for ten days when the harvest was to begin. At last Rodmika could be spared for a long trip into the jungle. Little preparation for such a trip was necessary; a small bag of rice, a tin of salt, a cooking pot, his sheath knife and fire striker were quickly assembled. He knew, too, where to find additional food in the jungle. There were the tender green shoots of the nettle, and fish to be trapped with his hands beneath rocks and among the submerged roots of trees.

In the starlit darkness before dawn the next morning when he sat up on his cot he saw a vague moving shadow upon Dobarra's cot. Then he recognized the familiar movements of a small boy wrapping a white turban snugly about his head.

"Now what, little monkey," whispered Rodmika. "If thou has brewed plans to go into Green Jungle with me, then wipe them out and return to thy sleep."

Dobarra giggled and continued to swing the white cloth about his head. "I have matters to attend to in my own jungle," he said importantly, "but I shall go with thee to the edge of the great sunken land. Have no fear for me, brother, for I, too, am at home in the jungle."

They were soon upon the dim winding trail with dewy branches dragging wetly across their bare legs and chests. "If thou findest a trail to the Foundation mark it well so that I may go with thee to the school there," said Dobarra.

"It is twenty miles of water and jungle-covered islands," answered Rodmika. "We may never find a trail through it."

"But thou wilt try?"

"Yes, I will try."

"Then it will be found," Dobarra went on. "The *sahibs* at the Foundation will send their carts loaded with grain through Green Jungle to Kumba, and we shall go through the other way to school."

"They cannot build roads on water," said Rodmika. "It would be too costly to bring in earth and stone enough to make a twenty mile roadway rise above the swamp."

"But the grassland that the old one told thee of. Is it not dry land?"

"It may be, but who can tell how far it will reach. Perhaps only a mile or so. Then there is the monster."

"Ah yes, the monster," said Dobarra. "I would like to see a monster, but from a high tree."

"There may be no trees in the grassland," commented Rodmika.

"Ugh!" said Dobarra, drawing closer to his brother.

The trail that had at first climbed along the slope of the low hills now dropped suddenly into a mist-filled vale. The undergrowth became thicker and in the increasing light the broad leaves were greener than anything on the hills or beyond in the dry winter forest. Rodmika stopped, and for a moment the boys stood together listening to the waking sounds of the jungle.

"And thou wilt go into that alone," said Dobarra with a shudder.

"Run home, little monkey," said Rodmika.

"And wilt thou watch until I reach the top of the hill?"

"Yes, but run. It is growing light and I must be on my way."

* * *

Sunrise found Rodmika deeper in the sunken land than he had ever been before. The densely tangled islands were farther apart now. Travel through the trees and vines was becoming almost impossible. A dozen times he swam wide stretches of green water with his supplies on a small cane raft trailing behind him at the end of a vine which he held in his mouth.

Twice he saw the noses of crocodiles as they made V-shaped wakes on the surface as they followed him.

By noon Rodmika was as tired as if he had been traveling all day. He lay upon a bank beneath the giant canes of a bamboo clump, looking up through the criss-cross pattern at the cloudless sky. Here and there in the tangled mass above him a big cane had rotted away at its base and leaned upon its fellows for support. It set Rodmika thinking. Perhaps Vallabiah and Beg Mohammed, the village youths of long ago, had been wise in building a raft. Rodmika rubbed his sore muscles and considered the distance still ahead of him. It would be a longer trip on a raft, but he wouldn't have to swim in uncertain waters, nor would he have to struggle through the tangle of limbs and vines. He decided to build a raft.

Climbing into the bamboo clump, he tugged at the loose canes. They were all much too long to use as they were, and Rodmika knew that with only his small sheath knife he could not cut through the iron-hard fibers. But, still, he had another useful tool in fire.

He dragged two forty-foot poles to the bank and built a fire. Counting off ten joints from the big end of one, he placed the eleventh over the blaze and lay down to doze in the cool shade while it burned through.

He was drifting away in a dream of the other boys at the Foundation when the whole earth seemed to heave and blast him from his sleep with a thunderous roar. Fire and hot ashes rained upon him as he leaped in stunned confusion to his feet. Long shredded strips of split bamboo swirled about him like

broken strings from a *sihtar*. As his senses cleared he looked first to his provisions, which fortunately had not been damaged. Now he turned to where the fire had been. Only bare damp earth remained. He examined the long sharp-edged strips of bamboo trying to collect his reasoning. What had happened? What caused a forty-foot bamboo pole six inches in diameter to explode with a roar like Abdul's rifle? He seemed to hear Mrs. Towers, who had taught his class at the Foundation, saying, as she so often had said, "There is a reason for everything. Nothing happens without a reason. And usually that reason is very simple and easy to find if we will only look for it."

Rodmika tried to reason. The startled feeling still tingled over his skin and at the roots of his hair. He took out his fire striker and kindled a new blaze with a handful of dry brush. Carefully he examined a piece of the bamboo that had lain in the fire. To his surprise he found that it was hardly burned at all. He placed it in the flames and watched. Slowly it now took fire and burned with ease. That was all. He selected a short length of small bamboo and cautiously thrust it into the fire.

It gradually lost its green color and became a smoky brown. Then just as the big one had done, it split from end to end with a vicious snap. Wonder grew deeper on Rodmika's face. He reached for another piece of bamboo and examined it closely. "Yes, ma'am," he said as if speaking to Mrs. Towers, "I will look for the reason. The cane exploded. For anything to explode in fire it must have something in it which fire compels to get out. But a cane has nothing in it. Everyone knows a cane is hollow. That's why it floats so well. Still, it explodes in fire. There must be something in it." He was thinking hard.

Drawing out his knife, he forced the point of it through the tough fiber of a small bamboo staff and again placed it in the fire. Again the green changed to brown. Rodmika shielded his face with his hand and awaited the explosion. None came. Instead, a hissing sound came from the cane and he saw a small jet of steam issuing from the slit his knife had made.

"Aye," he said, "so that is the reason. The hard polished surface of the cane kept the moisture in. The fire turned it to steam and the steam had to get out. Steam caused the explosion."

He turned attention again to the large bamboo. He counted off ten joints. Then with his knife he drilled a hole in the eleventh for the steam to escape and placed it on the fire. He had no more trouble after that in burning bamboo in two.

With four ten-joint lengths laid out side by side upon the bank he placed short lengths of split bamboo across them and bound them all together with creepers. It made a strong raft ten feet long and some two feet wide which floated high with Rodmika's light weight. He shoved the raft off into the black lagoon, using a bamboo staff to pole his craft over the shallow waters. His spirits were higher now. Although the way would be longer, he could move faster. He wondered now why he hadn't decided on a raft sooner.

Animals looked at him in wonder as he glided silently past. Deer and nilgai turned their heads from their browsing, shook their big ears, one at a time, and stared. Once a pair of hyenas drew in their panting tongues and sniffed the air in their nervous fashion. Monkeys chattered, parrots screamed, and from high overhead the whistle of great eagles came softly down to him.

Occasionally throughout the afternoon Rodmika sought out a spot where the sun came through the foliage. As he poled through it he studied where his shadow lay and corrected his course. But as the sun dipped lower in the west he could see only where it brushed with gold the uppermost boughs of the trees and he grew uncertain of his direction. He was about to stop and make camp for the night when a low whirr came to his ears, and in the next instant the rush of birds was overhead. They came directly toward him, telling him that his course was true. The grasslands lay straight ahead.

. He poled on until the sun had set and pushed ashore to prepare his evening meal. With darkness over the jungle there came silence—silence so profound that it would make a village dweller's ears ache. When he had finished eating, Rodmika lay upon his bed of dry reeds, soaking in the beauty of the stillness until at last he fell asleep.

T NOON THE next day Rodmika slid his raft up on the mud bank of a narrow back-water stream that cut its way into the grassland. A lone curlew flew low over the water following the winding course. At the top of the bank the grass, taller than a man could reach, was parted by an animal trail. Many tracks came down into the water and emerged on the other side of the narrow stream. Rodmika climbed the bank and went a little way along the trail, examining the tracks. Among the hoofprints of deer, pig, nilgai, and buffalo he found the pug marks of two tigers and a leopard. Here and there, almost lost beneath the cutting hoof prints, were also the tracks of an elephant. He searched on, looking for something he did not find—the tracks of Gonda, the monster of the grasslands.

Returning to the raft, he poled back to the edge of the forest and climbed a tall teak tree that looked out over the wide expanse of grass. Far away in the rising blue vapor he could see again the dark line of the forest. The grass jungle was about three miles across, he guessed, and was completely circled by the towering forest. Here and there back-water channels cut through it to form an open lake in the center. Clouds of birds rose and settled back. Gray herons and white egrets seemed constantly on the wing, but he looked in vain for the monster.

The animals with which he was familiar would be bedded down during the heat of the day. Perhaps the monster was such an animal! Vallabiah had mentioned its hard hairless shoulder. Rodmika could think of only two such animals: the elephant and the wild buffalo. But either one of those, Vallabiah or any other village youth would have recognized.

While still in the tree he laid his plans for searching the grassland for the pavement or the remains of the lost city. Nothing showed above the grass except an occasional clump of trees. In the distant blue wall of the forest there was one point where the trees seemed to grow on higher ground. After searching the grassland he would go there.

But first, he decided, he would pole his raft through to the lake and investigate all the little back-water creeks that opened into it.

* * *

When Rodmika reached the lake he found it to be about half a mile across and circular in shape. It had no regularly defined banks, but he could see by the changing nature of the grass where the land sloped into the water. As the lake gradually became too deep for the reeds and grasses, lily pads and lotus blossoms covered the surface. Farther out the deep water rocked with small waves and was clear except for a group of pintails that paddled nervously ahead of Rodmika's raft.

He passed several small inlets and came to another, wider than the rest. His heart leaped at the sight of it. It was as straight as an arrow; and Nature, Rodmika knew, made few things straight. The straightness of this wide creek, somehow, had the mark of man about it. The boy paddled into it, study-

ing the low banks on either side. Animal trails broke through the grass at frequent intervals. Occasionally there were mud wallows which he knew were used by both wild buffaloes and elephants.

69

Two cheetal came out of the grass and down to the water's edge to drink. Rodmika felt better in their presence. They were the first animals he had seen in the grassland.

Suddenly with a whirr of wings a brace of swamp partridge rose above the grass. In startled flight they separated and veered sharply down into the jungle.

"Jungli *teetar*," whispered Rodmika musically as he recognized the birds. He rested his pole across his knees and watched the deer. As he expected, they became anxious and a second later bounded back into the grass.

"The *teetar* warned them," said the boy under his breath. Grass plumes waved violently and he heard a heavy body thrusting the tall stalks aside. "Perhaps it is the monster," he added poling his raft further from the shore.

Darkly through the veil of grass he saw a moving form. It was still for a moment; then with a rush it charged out on the bank, tossing two great scimitar-like horns.

Rodmika sighed with relief. It was a huge wild water buffalo. He stood knee deep in the mud with his nose out-stretched, testing the air with noisy snorts. "I would rather meet thee here," said the boy, "than on a narrow trail in thy jungle." There was no animal in India bolder than the wild buffalo, and none so likely to make an unprovoked attack. Rodmika avoided its haunts as much as possible. "Go thy way," he said, "and I'll go mine."

Rodmika dipped his pole into the water and pushed on up the straight channel. Ahead of him, extending upward from the black mud of the right bank like a dark trunk of a tree, was an immobile object as high as the highest grass plumes. Several long-legged white birds stood upon it. Rodmika poled toward it cautiously. He now suspected almost everything dark and large of being the monster.

The birds winged leisurely away as he came near. What they had rested upon seemed a dense matting of vines. A few feet into the grass he saw a similar projection. He thrust his pole through the vines, and it stopped with the shock of solid stone. Drawing nearer, he pulled the vines apart and peered at the moss-covered stone. He saw where two great squared stone slabs had been forced apart by roots grown to the size of a man's arm. With the point of the sheath knife he scraped away the moss and traced out a symbol that remained dimly in the surface.

"The same!" he shouted in excitement. "The same carvings that are around the doors and windows of our home!" He replaced his knife and climbed to the top of the ancient wall. He knew it was much higher than it originally had been for in places there was a foot of roots between stones that had once rested one upon another.

Rodmika looked down into the grass jungle below him. Scattered about for some thirty feet were large blocks of the same stone. His eyes searched for one familiar shape—the stone lintel that formed the top of the doorway. Upon that he was sure would be carved the cobra crown. He looked in vain. Nowhere did he see anything that resembled the lintel.

Before coming down he surveyed again the expanse of grass,

paying especial attention to the isolated clumps of trees here and there. The nearest was about three hundred feet away. Around it there seemed to be a small clearing in the grass. He decided to visit the clearing, and since it was growing late, he might spend the night there among the trees.

Returning to his raft, he pulled it high onto the bank and with his provisions he set out along a trail for the trees. He had no difficulty in reaching the place. Every trail in the neighborhood seemed to lead toward the clearing.

As the grass thinned out he stopped to study what lay before him. There was a sink in the middle of the clearing with a pond some fifty feet across at the bottom of it. A small she-elephant with her calf was emerging from it on the other side after a bath.

The ground about the pond was crusted with a white substance. Rodmika knew then why so many trails led to the clearing—it was a salt lick.

Para, the small hog deer with her spotted fawn licked the white stuff not far from the elephants; then suddenly seeming to sense danger they ran awkwardly to the grass and disappeared. Rodmika waited until the elephants, too, had vanished and trotted quickly across the bare crunching ground to the trees that grew at the edge of the sink.

As he approached the trees an astonished hyena leaped from the dry brush at their roots and fled panic-stricken for the tall grass. Rodmika checked himself in momentary fright. "Take command of thy senses, little brother," he said to himself, "that beast might have been a tiger or a leopard. What would it gain thee to rush headlong for the safety of trees when the monster himself may await thee there."

Regaining his caution he reached a heavy limbed *sal* tree in the midst of the clump. In the top of it was an abandoned eagle's nest of which Rodmika took possession. Since it was built with reeds and small sticks he found it not too uncomfortable. It gave him a good view of the pond and most of the clearing.

As he ate his evening meal of rice balls, cooked that morning, the sun became a blood-red disk, distorted and dimmed by the low-hanging vapors over Hara Daldal. The animals of the jungle began to awaken as the small birds swept away to the hills.

A peacock followed by three hens trotted from the jungle to the pond. Hardly had they satisfied their thirst when the alert cock bird gave the alarm call. "Kok, kok, kok," he cried, and with a powerful flourish of wings all four flew up into the trees to settle below Rodmika. The boy scanned the rim of the grass. Presently a leopard followed by its mate walked into the clearing.

Abruptly both animals crouched. Rodmika was then conscious of movement below him, as something walked. Its footsteps broke through the light crust at every step. It was still hidden by the foliage below him, but it was going to the pond. Rodmika waited, his heart pounding and streams of sweat running down into his eyes.

The leopards crept forward and stopped again as a great blood-chilling roar burst from the creature below. There was

73

a familiar sound in that roar, but Rodmika was so determined that he was about to see the monster of the grasslands that he failed to recognize it.

The sun had set and the brief twilight was rapidly waning. In another instant the animal below appeared. Although it was the biggest tiger he had ever seen, a wave of disappointment and contempt swept over him. "Only a tiger," he said to himself. The tiger roared again, and the leopards snarled before turning back toward the grass.

Darkness had settled over the sink before the tiger left. Rodmika looked up at the stars. They shone faintly through the heavy jungle vapor. "But the moon," whispered the boy, "it will be bright, and in two hours it will be up. For the rest of the night I shall then see all that come to the pond."

In the starlight Rodmika made out the massive forms of elephants and the lesser forms of buffalo as they came to drink and eat salt. He was even able to recognize the high-shouldered nilgai, the horse-like antelope with spike horns that came in a drove of eight. The pigs he recognized by their grunting and squealing.

When the moon rose it was the same thing over again, it seemed, and after a while he grew weary of watching and fell asleep. However he was awake before dawn and had a cooking fire going at the foot of the trees. The sun was just rising above the distant hills when he gathered up his bundle and took his cooking pot to the pond to wash it. The first rays of the golden warmth were welcome upon his back as he squatted, rubbing sand into the brass vessel.

Suddenly the warmth was gone. He was cloaked in a chilling shadow. Lifting his eyes he looked across the pond to where the low sun threw the outline of a great, ponderously-moving beast. Hathi, the elephant, was Rodmika's first thought. Unless it was a bull gone mad there would be no danger. He took up his things and turned about.

Silhouetted against the sun the creature seemed to be a giant pig, bigger than the biggest water buffalo. Yet it was not like a pig nor like any other animal he had ever seen.

It stopped, threw up its small head and snorted. Rodmika gasped when he saw that a horn the length of a man's arm grew from its nose. The creature came on slowly, cautiously. The boy seemed rooted to the muddy brink of the pond. All the stories he'd ever heard of demons came flooding into his mind, yet it was no demon. It was Gonda, the monster of the grassland. The gentle morning breeze came down the slope to Rodmika, defying the animal's effort to scent him.

Rodmika fought the paralyzing fear that held him rigid. If one were to survive in the jungle, fear had to be replaced with action. Thoughts flew quickly through his mind. In one flash he recalled a mouse deer he had once seen held in a deadly trance by the presence of a python. In another he saw Boda, his father's work buffalo, and a goat at the Foundation. The buffalo and the goat had been friends since the goat was born; yet when the goat walked about on its hind legs beneath a banyan tree, nibbling at the air-roots dangling from above, the buffalo became enraged and charged it furiously.

Only brief seconds these thoughts took. The monster stopped

and blew vapor from its nostrils. It stamped a forefoot that shook the ground. Now it was acting like an animal. Without his conscious direction Rodmika's thoughts raced back over the same pattern. He had clapped his hand to break the trance which held the mouse deer, and it dashed away just as the python launched its javelin-like nose. And the goat learned never to walk on its hind legs in the presence of Boda.

Yes, the monster was acting like the other jungle animals. It would *walk* not another step forward as long as the strange little upright creature was there. From that point it would make up its mind either to charge or retreat—and so large an animal with such formidable armament would not likely retreat. There was no hand clap to break the boy's trance. It must be done by his own will. He must act, and act now. His pattern of thinking became his guide for doing.

Dropping down, he pressed one hand into the damp earth while the other gripped tighter his bundle. Then like a monkey mother holding her infant Rodmika hopped away toward the trees. He heard the crunch of the ponderous feet in the crust behind, and wanted to spring up and run, but he knew better. The animal could overtake him easily if it wanted to. He kept steadily on.

As he reached the crest of the sink, there was a splash in the pool. Rodmika turned to look. The great beast had dismissed from its mind the creature that walked on three legs. The boy crept to the trees and watched as the monster wallowed like a great pig in the mud.

"So, thou art Gonda," he said, when his courage returned. "A strange horned-nosed monster thou art, but still just a creature of the jungle, I can see."

Rodmika decided to go back to the raft before Gonda finished his bath. When he was again afloat in the straight water channel he looked back toward the lake. What he saw caused him to swing the raft about. Across the lake directly in line with the straight channel was the rise in the line of forest trees. "If the lost city be here in the grassland," he said, "then I shall never find it. The grassland is unfriendly and shelters strange beasts. Who knows what other queer creatures are here besides Gonda. But I don't think the Lost City is here. I think that this straight waterway is above the old highway. Those vine-covered stones were once a rest station beside it as perhaps our own home was also. I shall seek the Lost City in yonder forest. A forest is friendly. It is land that I understand."

S RODMIKA PADDLED his raft toward the forest across the lake, the rise of ground which he had noted from the straight water channel seemed to drop behind the nearer trees. A small inlet carried him through the narrow grassland that lay between the lake and the towering jungle.

A few minutes later he stepped from his raft into the friendly forest. Now to find where the ground rose. He climbed a tree and looked back across the lake to correct his course. The water channel with the stone ruin on its bank showed that he was only a little way off.

By mid-morning he reached the foot of a low hill and took a narrow trail that led upward along its side. Vegetation became thinner, and the rocks were almost bare of soil. The steep slope at his side was unusually smooth beneath its coating of dry moss. It seemed to be an old wall that had grown tired and had leaned over against the hillside to rest. In sudden excitement he tore away the moss with his hands. Beneath it were squared stones—the same stones he had found in the jungle, the same stones that were in his father's compound, and in some of the walls of Kumba village.

Rodmika crept forward to find where the wall ended. The

slope became steeper, and long ago the stones had slipped away to lie in a bramble-covered heap at the foot of the hill. Why should anyone wish to take stones from the ancient pavement and lay them against a sloping hillside? He followed it faster, his excitement growing.

The scar in the stony hill where the stones had lain climbed higher. It reached the top and lay level with all stones in place. Like a flash of light in his mind Rodmika knew now that he had found, not a wall, but the ancient highway itself. No man had laid the stones upon a hillside. They had been on a level roadway, and the convulsions of the earth had twisted it in every shape.

He eagerly followed the pavement, running where he could and impatiently climbing through a tangle of vines and creepers where the jungle had overcome it. As the hill became lower the vegetation became denser, and so progress was slower. At the foot of the hill the pavement was lost again beneath the deep black soil.

Rodmika took his bearings and worked on in a straight line. He hoped that he would find some trace of the paving stones where the ground rose. But in the next mile of travel he found nothing except the unending jungle. He was discouraged, tired, and thirsty. Although the ground was damp, he had struck no streams or pools since he found the hill. He was about to retrace his trail to where he had lost the pavement when a bull elephant trumpeted in the forest ahead of him. It was not a long screaming blast of rage, but short and more like a grunt of satisfaction. Rodmika glanced at the sun. It was past three o'clock.

Hathi would be finished with his rest now. He would feed until sunset, then he would drink. That's what a herd elephant would do, but this bull might be a solitary one, and there was no telling what a solitary bull might do.

The elephant trumpeted again. Licking his dry lips, Rodmika went toward it. It sounded as if he were wallowing in a pool or

Margaret Ayer.

a stream. He soon picked up a well-worn trail packed hard with the tread of heavy feet. Rodmika ran silently through the forest.

A moment later, to his great surprise he found that he was running along beside a stone wall some twelve or fifteen feet high. He checked himself quickly and stared through the vines that covered the carved stone blocks. The wall was crumbling at the top and at places was no higher than a man on horseback. At one point there had been a narrow gateway, but the lintel had given way and it was now filled with rubble. Beyond the wall he heard the elephant blowing water from his trunk. He continued cautiously along the trail, until he saw ahead of him a high opening in the wall. The trail turned into it.

A shadow darkened the opening as Rodmika neared it, and he instinctively turned aside and fled into the maze of roots of a giant banyan tree. He heard the elephant drag his sides against the opening as he came out and caught the pig-sty smell of him as he passed the tree, but he did not see the big bull.

When the elephant had gone, Rodmika crept again to the opening in the wall and looked in. At first the aged stone that met his eyes from behind the veil of jungle growth seemed a natural out-cropping of native rock. But the symmetry of the pile held his eye. It was like a confusion of great gray dominoes, some crushed and broken, and all traced with green moss. Without a doubt it was a temple or a palace of long ago. Here and there from the stones grew a large tree, a mango, a banyan, a teak, and beyond it all a cluster of palmyra palms held up their hand-shaped fronds.

He swept the wall-enclosed courtyard with measuring eyes. "Two acres and more," he said, and his farmer's heart noted the deep black soil and the little stream that flowed from the ruins of a stone-curbed tank of black water.

A strangely comfortable feeling came over Rodmika, a feeling of belonging to the deep black soil, a feeling of comradeship with the crumbling old stones. Almost fiercely he turned back to the opening in the wall and began to build a barricade in it against the return of the bull elephant. From the forest beyond he rolled short lengths of logs into it and criss-crossed the space above them with limbs and bamboo. The stone lintels above the opening had eroded away and the carved stone blocks above them hung precariously over the gateway. With a pole Rodmika prodded them, hoping to bring them all crashing down to close the entrance, but they would not move.

Reluctantly he left the gateway and investigated the tank. Two hundred feet long and half as wide, he decided, squatting on the curb and scooping up water in his cooking pot to drink. The water was clear and cool, but in its depth it seemed black. A great *cutla* swam lazily below him, feeding on the muddy bottom. The flash of red fins showed several small *rohu*. Rodmika licked his lips as he thought of one frying in *ghee*.

At the lower end of the tank the curb had crumbled away. The tracks of many animals in the muddy bank showed the tank to be the main watering place of the district.

"I shall call thee 'Kala tank,'" said Rodmika, "because thy waters are black." He turned now to the ancient building. Cautiously he worked his way around it. The sun had dropped to the treetops in the west and soon cobras would be searching for other serpents astir among the stones.

He found that there were four courtyards enclosed within the wall, but in only the first one was there a tank. The others were thickly overgrown with jungle, since there was no water in them to invite animals to keep the vegetation trampled down.

From the top of a palmyra palm he studied the center of the ruin and saw a dry fountain surrounded by a paved court. The many-columned cloister which had enclosed the court was a heap of broken stone on three sides, but on one side it seemed to be in a fair state of preservation, except for the chambers in the stories above. Monkeys seemed to be in full possession of the habitable portion of the ruin. They sat about the fountain, gazing uneasily at Rodmika as if he were some strange cousin threatening an invasion of their kingdom.

There was something about the ruined building that puzzled Rodmika, but for a while he couldn't decide what it was. He came down from the palm and examined the stones more closely. The columns of the cloister that still stood were cut to resemble wooden supports, and the cross members above were shaped as huge teak lintels would have been shaped.

He recalled what Vallabiah had said about the stone buildings of the early Hindus. They were wooden buildings made of stone. There were no rounded arches in wooden buildings, and there were no rounded arches here. All openings were flat-topped.

Whoever had built his father's house, he was sure had also

83

built this great palace in the jungle. It was the same workman-
ship, and the same designs carved about the windows and
doors.

Retracing his steps to the courtyard he added more poles to
his obstruction in the gateway, and looked around for a place
to build a small hut. A plan had already formed in Rodmika's
mind. He dropped to his knees and took up a handful of the
black soil and rubbed it between his fingers as it dropped back
to the ground. "A wonderful rice paddy this courtyard will
make when the monsoon rains come," he said.

That night he slept upon the broad crumbling top of the wall
that surrounded the courtyard, and the next day he built a hut
against the base of it. He thatched the roof with straw and wove
a straw matting for the sides. When it was done, he turned
again to the stone ruins. For two days he searched among the
carving for some sign of the seven-headed cobra. There was no
sign of the cobra crown.

It was now time to return home, but he was reluctant to leave
the courtyard. He walked about it examining the soil and
planning. "I shall build a *bund* here," he said, "so that the
water will flood my rice plants. I will need a plow and an
animal to draw it. Perhaps father will let me have Boda."

On his trip home, bearing in mind the thought of returning
with Boda, he sought to avoid the grassland and the lake. But
he was unsuccessful. He found that he must take a trail that
led for three miles through the tall grass. This would present
great dangers, not only to himself but to Boda as well. Rodmika
knew that there was a natural hatred that existed between tame

and wild buffalos, especially when the tame ones were found tethered or loaded with goods. Still he must bring Boda through the grassland if he were to take her to Kala tank and the ruins.

* * *

When he reached home there was so much work to be done that he had little time to discuss his adventures. His father, never much interested in the jungle, was too weary to listen, and his mother's fear of the dark swamp kept him from telling her much about it. Not even to Vallabiah was he able to relate his experiences, for on his next trip to the village he found that his teacher had gone on a journey to Delhi. It was only to Dobarra that he talked and told of his plans. Each night as they lay on their cots Dobarra begged to hear more.

"Take me with thee, O Brother," pleaded the younger boy. "I can drive Boda, plant the seed rice, and care for the young plants until we reset them in the courtyard paddy. I love the jungle, too. And I want to help find a way across the jungle."

"Sleep, little monkey," said Rodmika, "it is growing late." Rodmika smiled into the dark silence. It would be comforting to have a companion in the jungle. Dobarra was ten years old now and big and strong for his age. It was a happy thought, and with the smile still on his lips he fell asleep.

Nine

OW RODMIKA FOUND the courage to call at the strange old beggar's tumbled-down hut was something he didn't try to understand, especially after the conversation he had just heard in the village bazaar.

"Have we not beggars enough of our own?" complained Mucurgee, the flour merchant, as he measured out a *seer* of flour for the boy.

"It is true," replied the milk seller who had stopped to talk with Mucurgee. "Why should we give alms to one from so far away? Hast thou seen the card he carries about for people to read? It says that he does not speak our language and that he is returning to his home after making a pilgrimage to this country of ours. It asks nothing but food to sustain him on his long walk."

"That is fair," admitted Mucurgee, "we should feed pilgrims, but why does he linger here?"

"I think he brews some evil," answered the milk seller. "He has been tracing out lines upon a paper and peering about in our temples. I would speak to the wise one, Vallabiah, about him, but he is away in far-off Delhi for a time."

"That scheming wanderer will get no more flour from

86

me," snapped Mucurgee. "Let him be on his way or starve."

Rodmika took his bag of flour and walked aimlessly down the road. Vallabiah had been away since his return from the jungle, and he found that his trips to the village were dull and uninteresting. He continued to think of the old pilgrim and wondered why the two merchants were so resentful of the old one because he acted queerly.

"Good morning, my young friend," called a voice from a shop he was passing. The boy looked up to see sharp-nosed Motil Prinjrawalla, smiling at him from among the many cages which he had for sale. "Does my young friend know," said the cage seller, "that a fair is to be held on the village *miadan* the day following the morrow? Farmers from far and near will bring many things to sell. Does my young friend have something he would like to sell? Perhaps some pigeons, or a brace of quail or a jungle fowl he has trapped in the forest?"

"I trap wild things only when I am in the jungle and grow hungry," replied Rodmika, backing away a little. There were birds in many of the cages, and, towering over them, the grinning sharp-nosed Prinjrawalla looked as if he had once been a long-beaked bird himself. The man's voice reminded him of the cry of kites which now cast their circling shadows upon the sunny roadway. "But," the boy answered a moment later, "I do have two fine peacocks which I raised from tiny chicks."

"Splendid!" exclaimed the man, slyly rubbing his hands together. "Many peacocks will be brought to the fair, but they will be thrust into bags or merely have their feet tied together. They will be bruised, their feathers will be broken and their proud crests will be spoiled. They will look as though pariah dogs had chewed on them, and they will sell for the price of chickens. But not thy birds, my young friend."

Motil Prinjrawalla lifted down from its hook in the rafters a large red cage with bright brass wire handles. The boy looked at it with admiring eyes. Although he did not want to see his birds locked in a cage that was the best way he knew of displaying them at the fair.

At that moment another man spoke, and Rodmika turned to see tall, black-bearded Hassin, the bus driver, standing behind him. "A Parsee lady is coming to the fair in my bus," he announced, "and she is coming for no other purpose than to buy two fine peacocks for her compound. She will ask my judgment before she buys, and I certainly shall recommend none that have dirty or rumpled feathers."

"See, my young friend," said Prinjrawalla, pushing the cage forward. "Only in such a cage as this one can thy birds be safe from damage."

"How much for the cage, then?" asked Rodmika timidly.

"Eight rupees and four annas," answered the man, and added, "it's worth fifteen at least."

Rodmika's heart sank. He had only four annas, just one fourth of one rupee. "I don't have that much," he said. "I've never had so much money as that at one time in all my life."

"Then go back to the jungle and stop wasting my time," screamed the cage seller. Then to Hassin the bus driver, "See that. He leads me to believe that he will buy, then, verily, he says he has no money."

Hassin laughed, and Rodmika was glad to get away. He had almost reached his father's cart when he remembered the old pilgrim again. He hated to think of even an evil one starving.

A woman passed him, carrying a board upon her head, heaped high with dried fish. For half an anna he bought one of the fish, and for another half anna he bought a handful of rice from a farmer's cart. Then he went to the ruined hut where the old pilgrim lived.

In answer to his uncertain call, long thin fingers pulled aside the reeds that closed the doorway, and two strangely slanting eyes peered out from the dark interior.

"*Salaam,* O Grandfather," greeted Rodmika in the village dialect. "I have brought thee food."

The old man stared at him not understanding until he saw the fish and rice which the boy held out to him. A slow smile came over his wrinkled face and he extended one hand to take the food.

In his other hand he held a book which he quickly hid in the folds of his ragged robe when he saw Rodmika looking at it.

"You have an English Bible," stated the boy in English. "You must speak English." The old man looked at him in amazement.

"Please," he said with fear in his voice, "you must tell no one about my Bible."

"Don't worry," reassured Rodmika, "I shall say nothing. My father has an English Bible, too, but he makes no secret of it."

"Nor is he a ragged pilgrim far from home," commented the old man. "If those of the village learn that I possess so fine a book they will think I stole it, or at least, make me part with it to pay for food."

"Have no fear," returned Rodmika cheerfully. "You shall go with me to my father's house and stay until you have rested. I brought a bullock cartload of charcoal to the village and the cart will return empty save for us."

The old pilgrim gratefully accepted and while he cooked and ate his simple meal, Rodmika went to the village *miadan* for the bullock cart.

Jankari welcomed the old man heartily when they reached the forest homestead. When he saw his bruised bare feet he gave him some sandals he had just completed for himself.

* * *

That night after the pilgrim had gone to sleep Jankari shook his head and said to his family, "The old one is weak. If he is forced to continue his way on foot I am certain that he will never reach his home. It would be better if he were persuaded to remain with us."

"I shall ask him tomorrow," volunteered Rodmika.

But when he made the suggestion the next morning the old man stoutly asserted that in a few days he would be strong enough to resume his march. "My friends await my return to the North," he said. "I must not fail them." He deftly changed the subject, commenting upon the beauty of Rodmika's peacocks that strutted and preened themselves in the compound.

"Never have I seen such lovely peacocks," he said. "They should be taken to the fair which I was told is to be held on the village *miadan* tomorrow."

"I would like to take them," said Rodmika, "but I have no cage."

During the day he attempted to make a cage by weaving together long strips of bamboo as the old pilgrim looked on placidly. It was more like a basket than a cage, and when he put one of the frightened peacocks into it, the bird could hardly be seen, except for its long tail which had to stick out through an opening.

Rodmika was discouraged and abandoned the idea of going to the fair altogether.

* * *

He seemed hardly to have gone to sleep that night when he awoke at the sound of his name being called. The brilliant light of the late moon flooded the room, but it revealed no one but Dobarra sleeping soundly upon his own *charpoy*. Again his name was called, and this time he recognized the voice of his old friend. Looking out through the window he saw the pilgrim sitting against the post in the center of the moonlit threshing floor. Rodmika dressed quickly and went out.

"You called me, Grandfather?" asked the boy.

"Dawn will soon be breaking across the eastern sky," commented the old man with a wave of his arm, "and you have a long way to go to the fair."

"Go to the fair!" exclaimed the boy.

"Certainly. Fetch one of your birds."

Rodmika shot a questioning glance at the calm, confident old man, as he obeyed the instruction. Climbing into a tree where the peacocks roosted, he grasped the larger bird so that it could not struggle and returned to the threshing floor.

"Now, Grandfather," he asked, "how will I take them? Even a big cage is not good."

"You will need no cage," said the pilgrim. "Your peacocks will sit quietly upon a perch which you shall carry across your

shoulder. But, come, we are losing precious time. Hold the bird closer while I work."

Still puzzled, Rodmika watched the old pilgrim's sure fingers. From under one wing he drew out two long silky feathers.

"There," he said, "these feathers will hold this peacock more securely than a cage. Now, look carefully at the way a bird's eyelids work. See, they close by moving upward over the eye, and not downward as your eyelids do."

While the boy studied the peacock's eyes the pilgrim stripped the fringe from the feathers until they were like strings with hard points at one end and fluffy tassels at the other. "You will notice," continued the old man, "that a bird has no eyelashes, but instead has a hard thick rim. That rim has no more feeling in it than a fingernail. Now I press the point of the feather through the feelingless rim of each eyelid."

Rodmika watched as the feathers were drawn through the tough membrane until the tassels would let them go no farther.

"Now," said the pilgrim, "I bring the ends of the feathers up, pulling the eyelids over the eyes, and tie them gently over the head. The bird is blindfolded. Place it on the ground and fetch the other."

"But, Grandfather," protested Rodmika in alarm, "if I turn it loose it will thrash about and perhaps break a wing."

"Do as I say," commanded the pilgrim, chuckling good-naturedly.

Rodmika obeyed, and to his amazement the peacock stood perfectly still.

"Since he sees no better place to go," added the old man, "he stays where he is placed. After the fair the feathers can be clipped away and he will see as well as ever."

When the other bird was likewise blindfolded, Rodmika set about preparing breakfast for himself and the old man.

"How can I ever repay you for what you have taught me?" asked the boy as they began to eat.

"I am your debtor," said the pilgrim. "In a small way I have repaid you for your kindness."

The old man looked at the sky growing pale above the eastern treetops. "Hasten," he said. "You have a long way to go. Take that bamboo staff, lay it upon the ground, and place a bird upon either end. Then lift the staff and balance it across your shoulder. They will ride peacefully with you to the fair."

* * *

In spite of his early start it was mid-morning before Rodmika neared the village. As he turned from the jungle trail onto the highroad the driver of a covered camel cart hailed him in a strange tongue. Then, seeing that the boy did not understand, he repeated his words in Hindustani, "Where is this fair to be held, my lad?"

"Straight ahead to the *miadan*," answered Rodmika.

"For a moment I thought thou wert a lad from my own northern mountains," said the cart driver, "for nowhere else have I seen peafowl handled in such a manner. For two months I have been wearily upon the road and have heard not one word of my native language spoken."

There was something about the driver's slant eyes that reminded Rodmika of the old pilgrim, and he, too, was from the northern mountains. "Dost thou know an aged pilgrim who journeys by foot to Nana Tal?" asked the boy.

"I would that I did," replied the driver, "for the hills beyond Nana Tal are my home. As soon as I unload my goods at the village *godown* I begin my long return journey, and companionship would be welcome."

"Wouldst thou take a penniless pilgrim? He speaks thy language, I am certain."

At Rodmika's words the camel cart driver's face lighted up

momentarily, then darkened, and he shrugged his shoulders. "I am a poor man," he said, "and my wares will bring me little. I shall do well to feed myself and my camels on the trip."

"What are thy wares?" asked the boy.

The cart driver grinned. "Like thee, I am loaded down with peacocks." He laughed aloud at Rodmika's startled expression. "My peacocks come from the bazaars of Cawnpore and not the jungle. They are certified never to moult, never to awaken thee early in the morning with their cat-like screaming." He laughed anew. "Also they will not lay thee any eggs, nor can you serve them up in a curry. My peacocks are featherless creatures cast in brass and carved in wood."

In great relief Rodmika laughed with the driver, and their ways parted as they reached the edge of the village.

Rodmika walked with his peacocks through the crowded *miadan,* admiring the many things brought there for sale.

Nowhere did he see peacocks as fine as his own.

Firmly he resolved to use whatever money he got for them to buy food for the old pilgrim's return journey. Seeking the shade of a large banyan tree he bought a handful of monkey nuts and a cup of tea, and rested for an hour. When he went again into the crowd among the stalls he saw something above the heads of the people that made him catch his breath. Hanging from a frame over a bird seller's stall was the cage he had been shown two days before. Into it were crowded two large peacocks. The strangely familiar voice of a man was saying, "Not only two beautiful peacocks, lady, but a fine cage too." It was Motil Prinjrawalla.

"But I don't want a cage," protested the woman. "I want two peacocks for my compound."

"Thou must have a cage, too," insisted the sharp-nosed Motil. "How wouldst thou get two such birds home without a cage?"

Rodmika pressed forward to see if the woman were the Parsee lady that Hassin had mentioned. Then he heard her say, "Perhaps thou art right. How much for the cage and all?"

It *was* the Parsee lady who was about to buy the peacocks, but before the cage seller could answer her another voice spoke from the crowd. "Here, my lady," it said, "this lad has peacocks that need no cage."

At that moment Motil saw Rodmika and shouted furiously, "Go back to thy stall with those ugly jungle chickens."

"I have no stall," was Rodmika's frightened reply.

"Stop that boy," someone shouted. He tried to run, but almost immediately a big hand gripped his shoulder. It was Hassin.

"Here, little brother," he said, "take these five silver rupees and give me thy birds. A camel cart driver told me of thy clever way of handling peacocks. The Parsee lady shall have no others. And one thing more I almost forgot: the cart driver bids thee hasten to him at the village *godown*. He has made an unexpectedly fine bargain for his wares and wants to find a certain aged pilgrim who is journeying to the north."

So much good fortune at one time was more than Rodmika could stand. Five rupees for his peacocks was at least two more than he had hoped to get, and in addition the old pilgrim's safe journey home was assured. In spite of all he could do two big tears rolled down his cheeks, but nobody noticed them. The eyes of the crowd were on the two fine peacocks sitting so quietly on the perch that rested across the high shoulders of Hassin, the bus driver.

Ten

A MONTH PASSED, bringing the hot sultry days of May. Still Vallabiah had not returned from his journey, and Rodmika's many questions concerning the ruins at Kala tank had not been answered. Then came June, and the sky, though cloudless, lost its blue color and became gray. The sun shone down like a copper-red torch, drying the last water holes and stopping the little stream that watered their grain field.

But the grain had ripened and had been cut and threshed in May. There was little else to do now but prepare for the coming of the monsoon. In the edge of Hara Daldal where the water was lower than Rodmika had ever seen it, he prepared a bed of rice seedlings which he and Dobarra watched over day and night to protect it from birds and other animals.

After mid-June the heat seemed unbearable. Great cracks showed in the fields and a heavy steamy haze hung low over the land. Jackals howled crazily at night, and Rodmika saw a hyena running stupidly in circles on the Kumba road.

Then one day a ragged black cloud appeared in the Southwest, and a hot wind blew fitfully. That night the house shook with thunder, and lightning made it as bright as day. A few big drops of rain pattered into the thirsty dust.

With morning the great gray curtain of monsoon cloud moved from the distant sea to the jungle. From the roof of his father's house Rodmika watched it come as he repaired the thatch along the ridgepole. It was the last thing to be done in preparation for the three months' season of almost constant rain.

After nine sunny months the hard dry earth and all the creatures of the jungle eagerly awaited the first showers. Below in the compound Rodmika's mother and younger brother cleaned the seed rice which would soon be planted behind the newly repaired *bunds* in the little stream.

From the forest came the sound of his father's ax, as he cut and shaped a forked limb of strong teak, which was to be Rodmika's first plow. His parents had consented to his having a field of his own at Kala tank.

The rain brought early darkness to the little homestead, and as the family sat at their evening meal, Rodmika told of his plans for the growing season at Kala tank that would soon begin.

"I fear for thy being so long in the jungle alone," said his mother.

His father smiled. "I have no such fears," he said reassuringly. "He is now thirteen years old. Has he not spent most of his life in the jungle? Abdul, the pig hunter, tells me that few men have our son's knowledge of wild things."

"Being alone at night will not be pleasant," admitted Rodmika. "I would like to have some other companion beside Boda and the wild creatures."

"Yes," agreed his mother, "it would be good for thee to have a companion."

"Let me take Dobarra," said Rodmika quickly. "He loves the jungle, too, and I shall teach him all I have learned."

"Oh," gasped the mother, "he is still a baby."

"I am ten," protested Dobarra, "and I speak good English, too."

"Good English?" questioned his father. "Is good English necessary for the jungle?"

"When we find a road to the Foundation," said Dobarra eagerly, "I shall speak good English to the *sahibs* there."

"My sons, my sons," said the father laughing. "One seeks the mystery of his forefathers and the other seeks a way to cross the jungle. And both paths lie in the great sunken land. Go forth, my brave sons. Let nothing stop thee."

Tears were in the mother's eyes, but she said no more. Rodmika placed one hand upon hers. "We shall be safe enough," he said. "I have built a hut and thatched it well to keep out the rain. And the great wall will keep out the jungle creatures. The soil is rich there and we shall have many bags of rice from our field."

Next morning the clouds unexpectedly broke, and the sun shone through as the boys drove the heavily loaded Boda toward the green jungle. Dobarra had never spent a night away from his parents and his courage began to slip as they reached the edge of the dark, dripping forest. However he kept his feeling to himself lest Rodmika send him back home.

Even with heavy rains it would be several days before the

water began to rise. They would have ample time to reach Kala tank, but their progress was slow with the ponderous Boda. Much of the way they had to wade or swim, and only by constant effort were they able to keep their pack animal from lying down in the water.

By nightfall they reached the island where Rodmika had built his raft, on the first trip, but it was no longer an island. The water had dropped so low that the channels were, for the most part, only isolated pools. There were several showers during the night, but huddled beneath a canvas the boys kept dry.

The next day was sunny, and they reached the edge of the grasslands before the sun was lost in the cloudbanks low in the west.

"This is the end of the forest," announced Dobarra from a tree he had climbed. "The grass goes on and on until it is lost in the mist. Where do we go now?"

"Straight across," answered Rodmika, "until we reach the forest on the other side."

"Then let us hasten before the sun sets."

"Not today, little brother," said Rodmika. "It is dangerous to take Boda into the grasslands during the evening hours or early in the morning. There are great wild buffaloes there that would attack Boda and destroy her. Then there is the monster Gonda."

Dobarra climbed to the ground and began helping with the camp. "I heard thee tell father of Gonda. What is he like?"

"He is like no other animal of the jungle," answered Rodmika. "He is greater than the biggest buffalo, yet not so big as an elephant. And like an elephant he has a tusk. But only one, and it sticks from the end of its nose straight up like a flagpole."

"Didst thou tell Abdul, the pig hunter, about this creature?"

"I did. But he laughed and said that most assuredly there was no such animal."

"But thou hast seen it, brother."

"Yes. And long ago my teacher Vallabiah saw it in this very grassland."

"Then how will we escape it in crossing to the forest on the other side?" asked Dobarra.

"Since Gonda is an animal," said Rodmika thoughtfully, "I am trusting that it lives like the other animals of the grassland. The elephant, the buffalo, the deer, the pigs, all dislike the heat of mid-day. It is then that they seek some cool shade to lie down and rest. When the morning grows hot we will move. We should find few animals astir then."

* * *

It proved to be about as Rodmika had foreseen. They had gone across the grasslands the next morning and were half-way round the reedy fringe of the lake. They had encountered nothing but swarms of birds. The forest was but a little way beyond when Boda lifted her nose and sniffed the air. She stopped, and the two boys trotting at her heels stopped. Rodmika noticed that the air was drifting toward them from one side, therefore the unseen creature that Boda had scented was not on the trail ahead. Rodmika motioned to Dobarra and pointed to Boda. "Let me help thee up," he said. "Stand upon our possessions on Boda's back and tell me what thou canst see."

Rodmika watched Dobarra's face as he peered about above the tall tasseled grass. As he faced into the gentle breeze his small body stiffened, and his eyes opened wide. Then he dropped down and dived into his brother's arms. "I have seen it, I have seen it," he gasped hoarsely. "I have seen the monster. There were two of them lying like great stones beneath a tree. Then one stood up. The horn upon the nose! It was as thou said. What shall we do?"

"What is the monster doing?" asked Rodmika.

"He is standing still beneath the tree."

"Then," said Rodmika, "we shall continue on our way." He prodded Boda and they moved on along the narrow trail.

The afternoon grew cloudy and they heard showers sweeping through the forest at a distance. Rodmika urged Boda on at a faster gait. Still it was late afternoon and dark with the low-lying clouds when they came alongside the wall.

"Who made that wall and carved all those elephants and people in it?" asked Dobarra in wonder.

"Some old king long ago," answered his brother.

"Didst thou ever see that king, Rodmika?"

"No. It was so long ago that not even our grandfathers could recall the king, nor their grandfathers before them. There is no living remembrance of the old palace, much less the king who lived here."

"How do we get inside?" asked Dobarra.

"See that opening in the wall beyond us. That is the only

gateway left. The others have fallen in and filled the opening with crumbling stones."

"It looks as if that one might fall in soon," observed Dobarra.

"Look!" exclaimed the older boy, with alarm in his voice, "the poles I placed in the gateway have been removed."

"Perhaps the old king's grandsons have returned," said Dobarra.

"Nonsense. It was some animal. Here, help me clear out the passageway so that Boda can get through."

"I see wild elephant tracks going in," warned Dobarra.

"And there are fresher ones coming out," said Rodmika. "The elephant has gone."

Across the forest the dull roar of rain swept toward them. Rodmika urged Boda through the opening and across the courtyard.

"We got here just in time," said Dobarra as the first cold drops pelted down. "Where is the hut?"

Rodmika looked about as if searching for something. "It's gone," he said. "The old bull elephant has trampled down our hut and eaten the thatch."

Dobarra raked the cold rain from his bare arms and looked up at his brother. Rodmika would do something. He always did. He would have to get them and their supplies out of the driving rain. He pointed toward the ruins of the old palace, but Rodmika bit his lip and shook his head.

"I haven't examined those old chambers yet," he said. "They may not be safe."

"But we must get out of the rain," protested Dobarra, shivering.

Without replying Rodmika took up Boda's rope and led her toward the palace. As they approached an open doorway the buffalo stopped, threw up her head and snorted. The rain came down harder and the boy did his best to force her on, but without success. Giving the rope to Dobarra he walked cautiously toward the gloomy doorway. He could see nothing inside but a litter of twigs and dry leaves on the ancient marble floor. Far back in the room he finally made out some broken pillars and a crumbling passageway that indicated other chambers beyond.

Returning to Boda, he loosened the ropes that bound their load. The plow and the other implements and bags tumbled to the ground, and gently they lowered the earthen jars, baskets, and brass pots. When their supplies had been pushed into the dry interior, Rodmika was about to step inside when Boda snorted and stomped her foot again. And before he could come to Dobarra's assistance she had pulled the halter rope from his hands and dashed back the way they had come. Once through the gateway she plunged into the jungle and was lost from sight.

They had to follow her by tracks alone. Rodmika feared that she might return home and cause their parents to become alarmed, but fortunately they found her a short distance away browsing as if nothing had happened. She seemed to have forgotten her fright and permitted them to lead her back to the ruins.

This time Rodmika had Dobarra keep her farther away while he went inside to investigate. He drew out his fire striker, which was a short joint of small bamboo capped at each end with a nutshell and filled with thistledown. After removing one nutshell cap he held a piece of an old steel file against the down and struck it a hard, raking blow with a fragment of flint. Fiery sparks showered upon the down setting it afire. Carefully he blew upon it until he had ignited several dry twigs, and soon had a small crackling fire going on the stone floor. Holding a burning faggot above his head he searched the chamber but found nothing.

A moment later he was at Dobarra's shivering side. "Let me have the halter rope," he said.

"Take it, Brother, and let me run to the fire. It's growing dark and my teeth are chattering."

"Not yet," warned Rodmika. "Wait until we see what Boda tells us."

This time as the buffalo was led to the palace door she showed no sign of fear. She walked through the doorway as though she were entering a stable, but it did not relieve Rodmika's uneasiness. He knew the fire had overcome some of the animal smell, but that animal might still be lurking among the shadows. Boda walked calmly across the room peering into the farthest dark corner. Suddenly she snorted, lowered her head and charged with a bellow.

Rodmika saw the leaping form of an angry leopard, as it tried to avoid the scythe-like horns of the buffalo, but it was too late. With one sweep of her head Boda sent the spotted beast flying against the stone ceiling.

It dropped to the floor with fear in its wicked eyes, and in its small brain was only one thought—to escape the slashing hoofs

of the ponderous buffalo. Like a shadow it darted through the doorway, and Rodmika watched with satisfaction as it vanished in the curtain of rain.

"Come, little brother," he called. "There is one spotted cat that won't try to come back here again."

As they sat warm and dry at their meal of curried fowl, rice, and milk, the rain swirled down in the courtyard, and Rodmika explained how he would stack stones in the passageway to seal off the rest of the palace from their chamber.

Dobarra looked uncertainly into the shadows. Slowly a cloud of fear came over his face as he fixed his gaze on the dark passageway. "Rodmika," he gasped in a trembling voice. "I see shining eyes. They look upon us from the darkness."

Rodmika lifted a burning faggot from the fire and studied the creature in the shadows. Then he chuckled. "Now I am sure we shall be safe," he said. "Boda will let no big cat come near us in the night and this little gray mongoose will keep away the serpents."

"A mongoose!" exclaimed Dobarra, the tension subsiding from his voice. "Can I play with it as I do with my mongoose at home?"

"Go slowly, little brother," warned Rodmika. "A wild mongoose can be just as savage as another wild animal."

He picked up a chicken bone and tossed it toward the long-bodied little creature. The mongoose came out of the shadows and cautiously approached the bone, then pounced upon it and darted with it into the darkness.

"Will it come back?" asked Dobarra.

"I think so," replied Rodmika. "In case it does thou should have a dish of Boda's milk ready for it."

Dobarra got the milk and placed it where the mongoose had picked up the bone. "Now," he said, "we must be very quiet and still."

"No," said Rodmika, "not if we want it to get used to us. We must talk softly and move about slowly and tap gently upon a brass bowl. That will help the mongoose to get accustomed to the things we do and the sounds we make. But don't be impatient. It will take time."

When the mongoose did return it was still cautious, but it drank the milk. The boys talked in low tones and moved their hands purposefully about as the little animal licked its lips. It wasn't long before it ran about the chamber paying them no attention at all.

As the fire flickered out they lay down upon their blankets. Dobarra slipped one small hand about his brother's arm. It was so big and strong. "With thee," he said, sleepily, "I am not afraid. With Boda, and the mongoose we will be safe. And with solid stone walls about us I will listen to the rain and say, yes, we are still at home."

Eleven

IT WAS WASH day in Green Jungle. Rodmika and Dobarra squatted on the curb of Kala tank, pounding their white garments against the smooth stones, while the warm rain pelted down on their naked backs. A little stream of water ran off Dobarra's nose. He looked at his brother and grinned. A similar stream ran off Rodmika's nose, but he seemed not to notice it, for in his eyes was a look of grave concern.

"What worries thee, brother?" asked Dobarra.

Rodmika heard, but he seemed unable to tear himself away from the memory of the vision he had seen in the damp gray dawn. From the doorway of their chamber it had looked like a bent old man in a white shawl hurrying across the courtyard. He had seen it for only a second; then it had vanished among the broken stones of the ruin. But it had been no dream—he had actually seen it.

"Brother," asked Dobarra, touching his arm, "what is it?"

Rodmika tossed his wet head to keep his hair from hanging before his eyes. "I was thinking of two things that may prove to be dangerous to us," he said frankly.

"More dangers!" exclaimed Dobarra, casting an uneasy glance about the courtyard. "I thought we were rid of our dangers when we stacked the blocks in the passageway to close off the old palace from our room."

Rodmika smiled. "There are dangers everywhere in the jungle—always. No plant or animal in the jungle is ever free from dangers. Still, everything has some way of meeting those dangers."

"I don't understand," puzzled Dobarra, wringing the water from his *puggaree*. "Grass is in danger of being eaten by Boda, but what protection does it have?"

"Its heart is buried in the ground where Boda's tongue and teeth cannot reach," explained Rodmika. "It soon sprouts again. The cactus has thorns, and the trees have thick bark. Still, the mighty horns of the bison can rip through the bark. For every protection one thing has, another thing has a means of overcoming it. The deer has swift feet, but Cheetah the hunting leopard can overtake the fastest deer."

"What are these dangers that threaten us?" asked Dobarra.

"One," said Rodmika thoughtfully, "is something that seems to be a danger because I don't understand it. Just at dawn I saw it move from the courtyard into the ruins. It looked like an old man wrapped in a white shawl."

Dobarra's eyes opened wide. "Could it be the old king returned?" he asked.

"No," said Rodmika standing up. "Bring your wet clothes. We will hang them inside our chamber to dry."

As they arranged their clothes along a coconut fiber rope strung across the chamber, Dobarra spoke again. "Didst thou say *two* dangers, brother?"

"Yes," replied Rodmika. "There is another of a different sort. I was awakened in the night by a rumble that shook the whole palace and set sleepy monkeys chattering all over the place."

"Another earthquake?" asked Dobarra.

"I am not sure," said Rodmika, "but I don't think so. I think it might have been due to something we did. When we removed those marble blocks to seal up the passageway we may have weakened an old wall so much that it tumbled down. We must climb into the ruins above our room to make sure that it is not in danger of falling in also. And while we are at it we should explore the rest of the palace to see if there are other rooms which we could use if we should have to move from here."

"But," protested Dobarra, "all those higher parts of the palace are filled with monkeys."

"We might drive them out of one room if we needed it," said Rodmika. "First we must find the court with the fountain in it that I saw from the top of the palm. The cloister and the rooms on one side of the court still stand. We will begin our search there."

After an hour of climbing over the slippery, moss-covered jumble of fallen pillars they reached the court. A huge mango tree had grown up beside the fountain pushing aside the paving stones as if they had been pebbles. Dripping from the mouths of the stone tigers that stood in the center of the fountain was water from the monsoon rain that somehow had found its way through the ancient leaden ducts.

Monkeys chattered nervously as they entered the shelter of the cloister. They wandered down a long narrow gallery with rooms and apartments opening onto it from either side. They were all empty except for sticks, leaves, and grass strewn over the floor and packed behind stone brackets and projections near the ceiling where the monkeys had built dens.

Next they investigated the structure above their room and were glad to find it in no danger of falling in.

"Now," suggested Rodmika, "let's go down this old hallway and see what damage was done by those falling stones last night."

When they came to a turning at the end of the hall, they saw a heap of freshly broken slabs and blocks. Under the cave-like opening of the next chamber dust still hung in the air. So absorbed were they in this new destruction that they almost missed seeing where some of the stones had plunged through the old marble floor.

It was Dobarra who discovered it. "Look at this hole in the floor!" he exclaimed. "I can see things down there. The room is full of things."

Rodmika knelt beside his brother and together they peered into the gloom below. "It looks like a forgotten storeroom," said Rodmika, "one that the king forgot to empty when they abandoned the palace."

"Could we climb down there for a better look?" asked Dobarra.

"Yes, but keep watch for the black cobra. He likes such dark places."

"Always dangers," said Dobarra with a shiver.

They had gone only a short distance down over the broken

stones piled in the hole, when they saw movement in the darkness of the dungeon. A dim white form moved slowly through the gloom. Then like a puff of smoke it rose and vanished as it touched the ceiling.

Rodmika crouched and shielding his eyes from the light above, tried to get a clearer view of the strange sight.

"What is it?" asked Dobarra, clutching at the sash of his brother's *dhoti*.

"It is the same thing I saw early this morning," said Rodmika.

"I keep thinking that is the old king come back to protect his storeroom," whispered Dobarra, his teeth chattering. "Or maybe it is the ghost of the old king."

"I don't know what it is," said Rodmika sternly, "but thou canst forget both the king and his ghost. It is either a man or some creature whose ways we do not understand."

When they reached the floor of the dungeon they could see an opening in the wall near the ceiling where some stones had fallen out. "Either a man or an animal could have gone out there," said Rodmika. "He could have climbed on those things in the corner."

"What are those things in the corner?" asked Dobarra.

The boys stumbled forward over the tangle of trash on the floor. Rodmika tugged at the vague objects piled in the corner. One piece came away with the ring of thin metal. He took it to the light and examined it.

"Looks like a shield of some sort," he said. "It's made of copper and so thin it wouldn't give a soldier much protection."

He examined it more closely. "Now I see that it was a covering for a wooden shield, and the wood has all rotted away."

"Look at this," said Dobarra, lifting something from the floor. "A big ax blade. There are a lot of them, but they don't have any handles. And swords, lots of swords."

"This must have been the guards' room," said Rodmika. "The whole corner is piled with shields." He took the ax head from Dobarra and examined it. "Why, this is copper, too," he said in surprise, "and the swords are copper."

"And here is a copper chest," announced Dobarra. Already he was pounding on the lock with a copper spearhead.

"Stop," ordered Rodmika sharply. He knelt beside the smaller boy and moved his hands over the chest. "This does not belong to us, little brother. What right have we to break locks!"

"Thy hand shakes," said Dobarra, "and thy lips quiver. It makes me afraid to see fear in thine eyes."

"I *am* afraid," said Rodmika. He pointed to the end of a small chain of glistening gold that had slipped from under the lid. It was not a fragile chain such as a woman might wear about her neck, but one of coarse links that might have been used to fasten a soldier's tunic, and at the end was a golden image. Rodmika held it in his hand so that the feeble light could pick out the shape.

"Seven heads, is it not, little brother," said Rodmika breathlessly.

Dobarra counted, "*Ek, do, teen, char, panch, chhe, sat.* Yes, there are seven, and three coils with the tail making a hook at the bottom. The same as the mark upon thine and upon

116

father's chest. The same as the carving above the doorway of our house."

Rodmika gazed thoughtfully at the image. "Go into the jungle and seek thyself," he said in a whisper.

"What's that?" asked Dobarra.

"Only something which Vallabiah told me." Rodmika rose and wandered aimlessly about the room while Dobarra remained kneeling by the chest. A large copper plaque leaning against the wall caught his eye. He touched it. It, too, was thin, and seemed, also to have been fitted about a framework of wood. Moving nearer the light streaming down from above he examined the array of figures hammered so exquisitely into the soft metal. From the life-like features of the central figure he wiped away the green mold with his hand. It seemed to be a court scene with a king and child prince seated upon a cushioned dais and surrounded by courtiers. The king wore a handsome mustache that curled up at the ends, and upon the heads of both were turbans—no, not turbans. Rodmika looked closer; they wore the cobra crown. The boy suppressed a gasp of wonder and looked over his shoulder to see if Dobarra had noticed.

Carefully he rubbed away the green mold from the figure's naked chests and there minutely inscribed upon both king and prince was the sign of the cobra.

He rubbed the bared chests of the attendants. Not one carried the sign, nor did any of them wear the cobra crown. It was all clear to Rodmika now. It was a mark reserved for the king. Each king would place the mark upon the chest of his oldest son who would, in turn, become king and place the mark upon his son. He knew, now, that he had found himself—he was, after his father, the king of these broken stones, this sunken jungle, the black earth of the courtyard, the dark waters of Kala tank. He felt a sudden, fierce desire to keep it all a secret. If it were kept a secret it could never be taken from him. He looked about him, searching for a place to hide the key to his past which he held in his hand. In one place the stone blocks of the dungeon wall had separated as far as the width of a hand. Quickly he pushed the protesting metal plaque through it as far as his arm could reach, let it go, and heard it splash in water far below.

He would never have to see it again to know the truth. And it was his truth alone, his alone to pass on to his own son in the years ahead. Dobarra still bent over the chest.

At that moment the light from the hole in the floor above grew brighter. The boys looked questioningly at each other before they turned and looked up.

A glowing white figure squatted upon the floor above. It seemed to shine as a spear of sunlight filtered through the ruin to strike it. Rodmika blinked his eyes to shake off his reverie. Then he whistled softly. "A monkey, as white as cotton wool."

"And his eyes are as red as fire," added Dobarra. "I never saw one so big and so fierce." He turned to Rodmika and was surprised to see that the fear that showed in his brother's face a moment before was gone. His hand, too, was steady, and his lips were firm. Dobarra turned back to the snarling beast that blocked their way and was less afraid.

"A monkey is always a monkey," commented Rodmika, getting to his feet and advancing slowly. "And I know why he is so white and has red eyes. A man in the village has a jungle cat like that. Abdul told me that animals are sometimes born that way. Their red eyes are weak and can't stand much light. That is why the white monkey goes about before day, and likes to stay down here where it is dark. It was he that I saw in the early morning hours."

"How will we get him to go away?" asked Dobarra.

"Perhaps if we move boldly toward him he will leave. The monkey people are not very brave."

"Wait," said Dobarra, hanging back. "The chest with the chain in it. Are we going to leave it?"

"Yes, leave it and forget it."

Together they advanced up the rubble-filled slope that led through the hole in the floor, but the big monkey growled louder and did not retreat. Instead he leaned forward as if he were about to leap upon them.

"I have a sword," warned Dobarra, as if he expected the monkey to understand his threat. "He is not going to go just because we act boldly."

"Thou art right," admitted Rodmika. "I am going to try something else. I read a book at school about a sailor who frightened a great ape by hissing like Ajgar, the python."

Beyond the white monkey his gray family moved about over the higher stones chattering their approval of their leader's defiance. Rodmika drew in a deep breath and let it escape in a sharp hiss through his tight-closed teeth.

"It doesn't frighten him," whispered Dobarra. "He can see that thou art no serpent."

Rodmika hissed again louder and longer. The white monkey held his ground, but the chattering of the other monkeys grew to a wild scream as they raced in terror through the ruins, deserting their leader.

The white langur grew nervous. His growl changed to an excited jabber. Into his fiery eyes came doubt, then fear. Maybe his family were right; perhaps the hiss was coming from Ajgar. Finally he could stand it no longer and sprang away in frantic leaps after them.

The boys made their way out of the dungeon and quickly returned to the courtyard. The clouds parted briefly and the sun shone through. "We must work on our field," said Rodmika. "We forget that we are farmers."

ODMIKA TIED THE last rope to complete their *machan,* the swaying watchtower that stood upon its four long bamboo legs high above their rice field.

Ten feet below him, squatting on an earthen *bund* at the edge of the flooded field, was Dobarra beneath his rain cape of big leaves.

"Will August never come?" he asked complainingly as a fresh shower swept the paddy field.

"It is August now," replied Rodmika. "Four days of August have passed already."

"Then why do we see no blue sky nor sunshine?"

"That will come in a few days more," said Rodmika, "on the feast day of Ganesha, the elephant god. Rain brings good luck, they say, on that day."

"The rains break off on that day?" asked Dobarra.

"Sometimes they begin to break even sooner," answered the older boy, "but we shall have showers throughout August and most of September."

"I wish that I had the power to stop the monsoon now," said Dobarra. "I've had enough."

"We should be thankful for a long monsoon," advised Rodmika. "It would make the rice crops better all over the country. But don't worry. It will end soon enough. Then the sun will begin to ripen our grain, and one of us will have to sit up here in the *machan* all day to frighten away the birds. Already I see signs of the clouds breaking. In a few days they will begin drifting back toward the sea, to await another year. What ails thee, little brother? Art thou homesick again? It has been only a week since we visited father and mother."

"Nay," said Dobarra. "I am sick of nothing but rain and the raids that Dukkra, the wild boar, makes on our field. I wish I had the power to make rain into sunshine and make Dukkra into a tree stump."

Rodmika laughed aloud and the echoes from his laughter rebounded from the walls of the old courtyard surrounding their field. "Shame on thee for thy crow thoughts, little brother. Neither Abdul the pig hunter, nor the *Sahibs* at the Foundation have wisdom enough to change the ways of nature without making things worse than they are. Even in using the small power which we have over nature we must be very careful lest we bring down misfortune upon us. It was by means of our power over nature that we made rice grow here in the court-yard. We can cut the sweet-tasting bud from the coconut palm, but alas, the palm dies, and we get no more coconut milk to drink nor oil to burn in our lamps."

"When shall we begin our search for the trail that leads to the Foundation?" asked Dobarra, glad to change the subject. "I had thy word that we would start as soon as the rains began to break."

"That day is not far off," said Rodmika, climbing down from the *machan*. "But we must make everything secure here before we leave, so that Dukkra cannot again lead his tribe through the gateway into our field."

"Dukkra is a coward," observed Dobarra, contempt in his voice. "He comes only when we are away or asleep. When he sees me wave my arms he runs as fast as he can. He and his whole family are afraid of me."

"Don't be misled," cautioned Rodmika. "Dukkra is truly one of the great and powerful beasts of the jungle. He runs from thee, because when he is not angry he likes to avoid trouble."

"I think that boar is in league with the white monkey," said Dobarra, with a joking grin upon his small brown face. "He gets the monkey to bring one of the old king's copper swords to cut the ropes that bind the poles in the gateway. For surely they look as if they had been cut through by a keen metal edge, and not bitten apart by teeth."

"Dukkra needs no help from anyone when it comes to cutting ropes," said Rodmika. "He carries his own swords with him. His long curved ivory tusks have an edge as sharp as my sheath knife. He can cut ropes and sticks as easily as snipping threads."

"There, the sun is peeping through," shouted Dobarra, jumping up in delight. "Let's get more stout poles for the gateway. Poles that Dukkra can't root under nor cut through. Then we can begin our search for the trail. Dost thou think we could begin our hunt for the trail today, Rodmika?"

* * *

The clouds soon closed in again, and for the next few days the rain swept down harder than ever. The boys kept close to the old palace. While Dobarra grumbled and fretted, Rodmika found his thoughts returning almost constantly to the old dungeon and the copper plaque with the court scene upon it. He would lie upon his blanket with his eyes shut and create visions of royalty in which he wore the cobra crown and kingly robes. In his dreams the old palace was restored to its former splendor, filled with bowing courtiers instead of scampering monkeys.

Once when he opened his eyes Dobarra was staring at him. "How canst thou smile and sigh with thine eyes closed? What goes on in thy mind to make thee so pleased while it rains and keeps us here?"

This didn't discourage Rodmika's dreaming. Even as he worked strengthening the bunds, or earthen dykes, in the rice field, he rode in fancy at the head of his knights, waving a copper sword. Without knowing it he began to lose interest in the rice field. He grew to dislike the smell of the black earth and to see it smeared upon his hands and bare legs.

Dobarra noticed that he avoided getting his feet muddy, and complained, "Art thou too good for the black earth that grows our grain?"

Rodmika grinned shamefacedly and tried to put his mind to farming.

Then on the day of Ganesha the sun rose in a sky almost clear. Before it was above the highest jungle trees the boys were on their way. They followed an animal trail that led along the low ridge beyond the palace. Now and then paving stones showed through the dense carpet of the sodden jungle floor, showing them to be on an ancient highway which led toward the palace from another direction. On each side the forest grew thick, and the overhanging limbs interlaced their branches above the trail, darkening it.

Ahead of them a peacock screamed, and its call was echoed by others farther away. From their right came the alarmed "tonk" of a sambur stag. A moment later the crashing of brush told them that the large elk-like animal was fleeing wildly through the thicket, coming directly toward them.

"Get some stones," instructed Rodmika. "That sambur is being chased by red dogs."

"What are red dogs?" asked Dobarra as he began looking for stones.

"They are small dog-like wolves," explained Rodmika. "They are the cruelest killers in the jungle. They are red everywhere except for the black tips of their tails."

"Will they not attack us," asked Dobarra, "as the great gray wolf would?"

"Nay, little brother, they fear man. Now, be ready with thy stones. When the stag dashes by, the dogs will soon follow. Jump in front of them and pelt them with stones to turn them aside. There! Quickly!"

In one great bound the sambur cleared the trail and was lost from sight on the opposite side. When a pair of panting red dogs plunged into the trail a moment later they were met with a shower of well-aimed stones which sent them scurrying back the way they had come.

"There," said Rodmika, "we have saved one animal from them anyway."

"I wish I could change all red dogs into paving stones," shouted Dobarra, flinging the last of his stones at the retreating animals, "then I would walk upon their heads."

"Be careful of thy rash wishing," warned Rodmika, "and save thy breath for the long trek ahead of us."

After several more miles the ridge became lower and the ground grew swampy. "I see water ahead," said Dobarra. "The old roadway goes down into it, and I can't see where it comes up again. Dost thou think we can go farther?"

"I will see," answered Rodmika. "Wait here while I climb through the trees to find how far it is to the other side."

As Rodmika worked across the jungle bridge of vine-hung limbs and thorny branches, he paused occasionally to study the still water below him. In places where the sun came through the foliage he could see the pavement among the water weeds on the shallow bottom. Schools of fish swam above it as though it were their highway and once the boy saw Mugger, the crocodile, glide gracefully across it, moving his long tail like a flag waving in a gentle breeze.

Ahead of Rodmika the water became shallower, and the roadway climbed over a small wooded island, then sank again below the tangled surface farther on. But the end of the swamp was near. Through the trees he could see the crest of a low ridge and in a few minutes looked down upon the shore where the pavement followed the land.

From the trees he could see in the mud at the water's edge strangely familiar tracks that showed where a large animal had come down the roadway and turned back. There were tracks he had never come across before in Green Jungle. Then another thing caught his eye; something shiny and metallic glistened in the mud near the tracks.

When he was about to go down for a closer look a shrill squeal came through the trees from behind him. It was faint and far away, but without hesitating a second he swung around and began racing across the limbs toward where he had left his little brother.

The squealing became more frantic, and Rodmika, striving desperately to increase his speed, slipped from a branch and fell toward the dark water. There was a splash as his feet plunged through the surface, but a sagging vine that had caught under one arm held and he slowly climbed back into the trees. After that he was more cautious.

As he drew near the land, he began calling as loud as he could, "Dobarra! Dobarra! Climb a tree! Quickly, climb a tree!"

There was little doubt in Rodmika's mind as to what had happened—his younger brother had captured a small wild pig. And now that he could see Dobarra even that doubt was removed. He was using a vine to tie up a squirming, squealing young animal. He had not heard Rodmika's warning.

Suddenly Dobarra jumped to his feet, shouting and waving

his arm in the air. Beyond him Rodmika saw the huge black form of Dukkra charging furiously, his white hooked tusks flashing in the late afternoon sun and the bristles on his back standing erect.

Rodmika dropped to the ground and sprinted for his brother, grasped him about the waist and swung him up to a low limb. As the savage boar charged beneath the tree Rodmika vaulted safely up beyond the reach of the slashing tusks.

"He didn't go away this time when I waved my arms at him," complained the trembling Dobarra in puzzled surprise. "And now, look at him. He is killing his own little pig."

Rodmika was too out of breath to say anything but, "Climb higher."

When they were settled in a cradle-like fork of the thick limbs, Rodmika spoke again. "The boar had to kill that pig. He had to stop that squealing to save the other young ones. Thou hast aroused the whole jungle. Every flesh-eating animal within hearing will think that there is a wounded pig abandoned by his family. They will come looking for it and also for the ones that are not squealing."

"What animals will come?" asked Dobarra.

"Thou shalt soon see," said Rodmika, his patience strained. "It grows late. All the animals are beginning to stir. Listen to that monkey's angry bark."

"It sounds like the white monkey," said Dobarra. "It barked and growled at us like that in the dungeon."

"It is just an ordinary monkey," explained Rodmika, "but it sees something that it fears. Now, there are others starting in

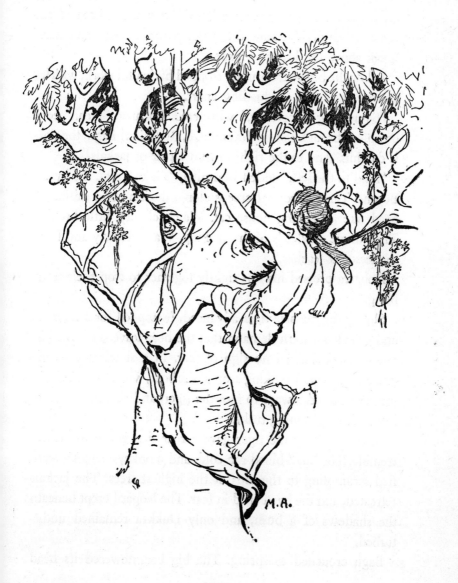

M.A.

all directions. And, look above. The long-winged kites and vultures are gathering, and so are the crows. Be still and don't speak above the lowest whisper."

Below the big boar abruptly stopped his brutal work, whirled around and gave a whistling snort.

"Something is coming," whispered Dobarra. "I can see it creeping through the shadows. Bagh, Rodmika! Bagh, the tiger is coming. And to the right of him a pair of jackals!"

"And to the left," added Rodmika, "slinks Tarsa, the hyena. Beyond Tarsa a leopard creeps along, ducking and raising its head like a thieving house cat. Watch closely, little brother. This jungle playlet is of thy making. Watch closely and learn the lesson it teaches."

Dobarra pressed his lips tightly together to stop their trembling.

Slowly the massive tiger advanced. It stopped for a moment and growled a stern demand that the boar leave the dead pig, but Dukkra showed no sign of fear. In a slowly narrowing circle Bagh began walking around the boar, which with its head lowered turned always to face the tiger, and snapped a warning with its gleaming tusks.

In rising anger the tiger gave a roar that made the leaves tremble. The boys' blood ran cold, and monkeys began a terrified scrambling to the tops of the highest trees. The jackals retreated, and the hyena fled in fear. The leopard crept beneath the shadows of a bush, and only Dukkra remained undisturbed.

Bagh crouched to spring. The big boar lowered its head

more, grunted, and glared defiance at the striped beast with its small fiery eyes.

The tiger's leap was like a tawny flash, but Dukkra was not taken by surprise. With an upward swing of his bristling head the boar ripped his attacker from shoulder to flank. Snarling in pain and fury the big cat slashed and struck the hog with both claws and teeth. The next instant the two brutes were a roaring squealing whirlwind of stripes, bristles, and torn earth.

Gradually the desperate struggle moved through the undergrowth to where the boys could no longer follow it with their eyes, but the noise of the battle rose to new heights of fury.

Silently the leopard crept toward the still form of the dead pig. A few steps at a time; then it would sink to the ground and look evilly about to make sure that no other tiger or boar was near. Two noisy crows, bolder than their fellows, swooped low over the pig. One alighted upon it for an instant, but flew screaming away when it saw the leopard. After one last cautious glance toward the fighting beasts the slim, spotted cat sprang upon the lifeless pig, lifted it in its mouth and darted swiftly away into the jungle. The jackals and the hyena followed for a short distance, but returned when the roars of Bagh became gasps and the snorts of Dukkra grew fainter. They knew that such a battle could end only in the death of both the great beasts, and they licked their lips at the prospect of a bigger meal than would be provided by the bones of one small pig.

It was growing dark when at last the jungle became quiet. Dobarra turned his face up to Rodmika. He opened his mouth to speak, but the words would not come.

The older boy smiled a little and said, "Don't feel too bad, little brother. I know thy thoughts. But thou must remember that jungle animals live in a cruel world. Having no love nor understanding for those outside their own families, they fight, and fighting, lose not only what they fight for, but their lives as well."

"Now," Rodmika continued as he led the way to the ground, "we must return to the palace and make a new start for the Foundation another day."

Still Dobarra remained silent, and when they had gone a little way along the old pavement, Rodmika turned to him and asked, "Art thou not nursing thy fear too long?"

"Nay, brother," replied Dobarra humbly. "It is not fear. I am worried. My power over nature troubles me. Wilt thou teach me to use it wisely?"

ODMIKA AND DOBARRA were still two miles from the old palace when the face of the rising moon grew dim as a dark cloud swept across it. They walked on as fast as their tired legs and the ancient overgrown paving stones would let them.

"I hear rain coming," announced Dobarra, stopping a moment to listen to the soft roar sweeping through the forest. "Can't we wait in a hollow tree until it passes?"

"I'd rather get wet," said Rodmika, "than risk being trapped in a hollow tree by Bhalu, the bear. He is near here now. A moment ago I heard him sucking white ants from their nest in a fallen log."

"Is there no shorter path we could take to the courtyard? I am tired and I don't want to get wet."

"There is a trail across the soft ground below the ridge," suggested Rodmika. "We would be spared a half mile by going that way, but it will not save us from getting wet. The rain is almost upon us now."

The rain came down with a roar, drenched them to the skin, and was gone by the time they reached the low ground. They squeezed the water from their clothing as best they could and quickened their pace. Before them the soft earth was covered with small pools. In places the trail formed the bed of a flood stream. The two hurried along.

"I am thankful that there are no more clouds in sight," said Dobarra. "I don't want to get wet again tonight."

"Hast thou forgotten?" said Rodmika. "This is the feast day of Ganesha. Good old Ganpatti. It is the day of the happy elephant god. It is lucky to be rained on this day."

"I remember," said Dobarra, laughing. "At the Foundation last year we threw a clay image of Ganpatti into the tank, and Towers *sahib* said it was heathen. But father winked his eye and said that a little Ganesha celebration wouldn't do a Christian any harm."

Dobarra ran splashing ahead in an effort to get warm. When he was some ten yards beyond his brother he gave a sudden startled shout and vanished from the open trail in a spray of water.

Rodmika leaped forward, straining his eyes for some trace of his little brother. But the uncertain moonlight revealed nothing until he was almost upon him. At his feet a sputtering coughing Dobarra was standing shoulder-deep in a water-filled hole.

"Now I'm wet again," he wailed.

Before Rodmika could pull him out, he too stepped into a similar hole.

"Who dug these holes in the trail?" grumbled the younger boy struggling onto harder ground.

"Take care," warned Rodmika, "there may be others. We must follow them to where there is less water."

"Follow holes!" exclaimed Dobarra. "What strange thing wilt thou say next!"

"These holes," said Rodmika, patiently, "are the tracks of Hathi, the elephant. But I have never seen elephant tracks so large except in our courtyard. We will follow them to firmer ground where I can measure them."

"Why do that?" complained Dobarra. "That won't help me get to the palace and my warm blanket."

"No," admitted Rodmika, "but it will tell us something about the Hathi that made the tracks. Never cross tracks in the jungle without learning all that they can tell thee."

After going a short distance Rodmika found a footprint that satisfied him. It was cleanly cut in firm ground. "Now, take thy turban and unwind it. It will serve better for measuring than mine, for I know it is two yards long."

"All right," agreed Dobarra, "but what is there to learn about a wandering bull elephant by measuring his footprint?"

Before Rodmika replied, he carefully laid the cloth around the rim of the big track. Then—"See, *baba,* thy six foot cloth will little more than reach around the front foot of this elephant. Since the one that used to bathe in Kala tank had the same measurement it may be the same animal."

"And that is not all," Rodmika continued. "Abdul says that twice around an elephant's front foot is equal to his height at the shoulder. This Hathi, then, is about eleven feet high. I never saw an elephant so high."

"How canst thou be sure that it is the front foot?" asked Dobarra.

"I can tell that," explained Rodmika, "by the marks of his ivory toenails. The front feet have five while the hind feet have only four. Now, let's get on to our chamber before something else happens.

* * *

They had hardly got to sleep two hours later when the sound of crashing timbers brought them rolling from their blankets. "What is it?" asked Dobarra gripping his brother's arm.

"I hope it is not what I think it is," replied Rodmika grimly, going to the door to look out. The moonlight on Kala tank showed Boda wading hurriedly out of the shallow end. She snorted excitedly and trotted into the deep shadows near the palace.

There was another crash of timbers and a huge dark shape filled the gateway in the wall.

"Quickly, Dobarra," directed Rodmika, stepping back into the room, "if we are to save our field we must not lose a minute. It is just as I feared. Hathi has returned. He is breaking through the barrier which we placed in the gateway. Empty the water from the big kerosene tin and fill it with dry leaves and sticks." He threw a blanket over his shoulder as he continued speaking. "Also bring thy fire striker and the bottle which holds the oil for our lamp."

When they were outside in the moonlight they saw the bull elephant force his mighty bulk through the ancient gateway.

"He is so big," gasped Dobarra.

As they crept along the palace wall toward the field, Rodmika explained further. "Like most of the animals of the

136

jungle, except the big cats, Hathi depends upon scents instead of movements and sounds to bring him information. He knows that noises and things that move are often one thing when they seem to be another. The smallest monkey can shake the leaves of the biggest tree, and a harmless green parrot can raise the echoes with its shrill cries. Hathi will believe only what his nose tells him. He seems to know that there are few false scents in nature."

"Then he may get our scent," ventured Dobarra.

Rodmika warned in a low whisper, "We must not let him. The man-scent is strange to him. It might arouse him to great anger. We must slip around the field until the breeze blows from him to us."

Stooping low, they kept close to the wall and crept through the tall grass that fringed the field to a point where the newly made *machan* was directly between them and the swaying elephant.

"Rodmika," whispered Dobarra, "I know not what thy plan is, but if it works, what is to keep Hathi from returning night after night until at last he has eaten all our rice? There is no way to keep him out."

"All that may be true," admitted the older boy. "Still we are not excused from doing our best tonight."

"Are we going to climb up on the wall?" asked Dobarra.

"Thy place will be upon the wall," replied Rodmika, "but I shall be in the *machan* with the kerosene tin. We have just one chance of success; we must give Hathi a surprise so great and so sudden that all judgment deserts him. He must suspect nothing until he comes into the field to eat our rice plants. When he gets near the tower I shall shout and beat upon the kerosene tin. That will be thy signal. Upon the wall keep low among the vines, light a fire and feed it with oil. Use this blanket to make a hood for the fire, and let not one ray of light reach the field until my signal."

"I fear for thee, brother," said Dobarra, trembling. "Hathi could crush that tower with one sweep of his mighty trunk. Hast thou frightened elephants before?"

"No," answered his brother, "but I know that they are sometimes very timid. And I remember a story Father told me about the ancient emperor Gupta. When Gupta went with a hundred war elephants leading a thousand soldiers to conquer a rebellious city, the people of the city hurled fire pots at the elephants, frightening them so that they turned about and fled, trampling many of Gupta's own soldiers.

"Now climb to the top of the wall and tell me what Hathi is doing. I will hand up thy things."

A moment later Dobarra called down in a low voice, "He is near Kala tank, searching the bushes for wild plantains."

"Get busy with thy fire kindling," instructed Rodmika, "and keep low among the vines. At my signal pull away the blanket and hold it so that fire shines upon it, and shout with all the power of thy lungs."

Feeling confident that Dobarra could be depended upon to do his part, Rodmika turned toward the *machan*. Holding the kerosene tin close to him he waded among the flooded plants until he came to the four long bamboo poles that made the

legs of the tower. Slowly he climbed up, pushed the tin onto the platform and pulled himself up after it. Then to his great surprise he saw Hathi standing in the edge of the field. Like a massive gray shadow in the moonlight he stood facing the *machan,* his trunk extended, feeling the air for some scent that would explain the reflections made by the moon on the shiny kerosene tin.

With a sucking noise he pulled one big foot after another out of the mud as he advanced. After a few steps he stopped, ripped up a bunch of rice plants with his trunk, and beat the roots against his knees to free them from the clinging wet soil.

Rodmika watched him as he ate the grass. The big bull was not angry or frightened, but he had grown suspicious. And Rodmika knew that a suspicious elephant could be very cunning.

When the great beast began moving again, it was not toward the watch-tower, but around the edge of the field near the wall, hunting for a place where the night breeze would bring him the scent of the strange object upon the top of the four swaying poles.

It was not long until he stood beneath the wall where the two boys had parted. Not six feet away from the high gray back Dobarra crouched among the vines that grew in a tangled mass on the wide top of the wall, but since his head was under the blanket tending the fire he knew nothing of the elephant's nearness.

Rodmika breathed in relief as the slight breeze died away,

but Hathi held his trunk high and continued sampling the air. The boy knew that any moment the breeze might spring up again. How different it was now from the way he had planned it. Everything was turned around. Instead of getting a sudden surprise, the elephant had turned hunter and was stalking him.

Hathi took a few steps toward the tower again as the air began to stir, then backed uncertainly to the wall. His big leaf-like ears extended wide from each side of his head and his long white tusks shone like sabers in the moonlight.

Rodmika was in a dangerous position and he knew it. If he could only get a signal to Dobarra! Now was the time for him to act. Anything to draw the elephant's attention away from the tower.

Rodmika saw the big trunk begin to coil as Hathi prepared for a charge. Then a faint choking cough came from the wall. It grew louder and Dobarra flung the blanket aside and stood up. A flash of light caught the elephant's eye and he whirled about to face the wall.

"Now!" shouted Rodmika, banging the kerosene tin with his fist.

Staggering about the wall, Dobarra was both blinded and choked by the smoke. He had no idea that Hathi was so near, but at his brother's signal he began to shout as best he could.

A sudden change in Dobarra's voice told Rodmika that he had at last seen the elephant. The small boy snatched up the blanket with one hand and a burning stick in the other. He flung the firebrand straight at Hathi's head.

The elephant lunged wildly to one side, lost his footing in

the mud and crashed down on one shoulder against the base of the wall. The whole courtyard shook with the impact of his six-ton body.

Rotting stones were dislodged from the wall beneath Dobarra's feet, and one large one bounded down upon the struggling elephant. Then came a shower of fire and screams. Dobarra went down with the crumbling edge of the wall and landed squarely upon Hathi's broad back. He slid to the ground as the elephant, trumpeting in panic, surged to his feet and plowed across the field toward the gateway.

The tower was directly in his path. As he struck the flimsy structure, poles, sticks, ropes, and a clanging kerosene can flew into the air. But Rodmika was not caught napping. When the elephant turned to the wall he slid to the ground and ran to one side of the field.

He now went to his little brother. Dobarra was knocking sparks from his scant clothing. "I'm on fire!" he shouted.

With one strong arm Rodmika swept him into the flooded rice field. The elephant reached the gateway and dashed heedlessly through it. There was a crunch of old stones, followed by a loud rumble. "Look," cried Rodmika, "Hathi has knocked the gateway down."

Dobarra stood up and wiped the muddy water from his face. "Thou hast made me all wet again," he wailed, "and it is nothing to shout about."

Rodmika smiled and placed one arm about his brother. "Forget thy miseries and look at the gateway. It is filled with stone. Neither Hathi nor Dukkra nor any other animal will get through there. No more must we come out into the wet night to drive them away."

"That's good," said Dobarra, still in a bad humor, "I'd not get wet again for all the good luck that Ganesha could give."

"Then run for shelter, little brother," said Rodmika, laughing. "It is beginning to rain again."

Fourteen

THE MOON WAS pale in the low, western sky when the first rose-colored rays of the rising sun touched the tops of the jungle trees. After their long, tiring climb through the vine-hung boughs in crossing the swamp, Rodmika and Dobarra dropped to the ground again. The older boy looked for the tracks he had seen at the water's edge two days before, but the rain had washed them away.

As Dobarra helped in the search, he found, not tracks, but a small silver disk which he picked up from the mud. Just as his hand touched it, something happened to drive all thought of both it and tracks from his mind.

From farther up the slope in the direction from which the old pavement led there came a piercing scream, which was repeated again and again. Dobarra watched his brother's face as they listened. It worried the younger boy to see Rodmika grow more puzzled each time the shrill cry was repeated.

"What is it?" asked Dobarra in a whisper.

"It is like no sound that I ever heard before," answered Rodmika. "But I need not know what it is to know that some creature is in terror."

"Perhaps we had better take to the trees again," suggested Dobarra.

"Perhaps we'd better find out what is happening," replied Rodmika and led the way along the pavement at a rapid trot. The screams soon stopped, but the boys did not slacken their pace until they came to the base of a low hill where the pavement ended in a circle.

After glancing quickly around the circle Rodmika dropped to one knee and examined some curious scratches on the paving stones. He pointed to them and said in a tone of uncertainty, "Those marks were made by steel struck against these stones with great force."

"What did it?" asked Dobarra.

"I don't know," answered his brother, wrinkling his brow. "All I can say is that a great struggle took place here, and not long ago either, for the steel particles scraped off onto the stone are not yet rusted. It must have happened at the time we heard the animal screaming."

Rodmika followed the marks off the pavement and into the jungle for a short distance. When he returned a moment later, Dobarra began asking him questions in an anxious voice.

"Is it wise for thee always to want to understand the strange things that happen in the jungle?" he began. "Dost thou never think of danger? Why can't we go on to the Foundation and leave the animals to settle their own quarrels?" It was not the danger that frightened Dobarra. It was the strange look that came into his brother's eyes. He had never seen such a troubled expression on his brother's face.

"I feel that we are really needed here," said Rodmika. "We must stay in spite of any danger." He pointed toward the jungle-clad hillside and added, "Dost thou see openings cut in the rocks?"

"Yes," answered Dobarra. "The shadows beneath the trees are dark, but among them I see carved doorways. It is a palace cut in the stone."

"Not a palace," corrected Rodmika. "It is an abandoned cave temple of ancient priests. I have seen others like it in the Ghong hills. There must be stone stairs beneath the brambles that lead up to it."

"Is that not blue smoke rising from one doorway?" asked Dobarra.

"So thou seest it, also," commented Rodmika. "It was so faint that I couldn't be sure."

"It means that people are here," whispered Dobarra, creeping closer to his brother.

"Yes," Rodmika went on, "but what kind of people. No people are known to live in Green Jungle."

"I am afraid," said Dobarra. "Perhaps those screams came from a man."

"Those screams," explained Rodmika, "came from the animal that made those marks on the paving stones."

"What other animal but man uses steel?" whispered Dobarra.

"The horse, for one," said Rodmika. "Those marks were made by a pony's shoes, and those screams came from a pony. Its tracks show plainly there in the jungle. I also found the print of a human hand in blood upon a stone. That is why we must stay and do what we can in spite of all danger. The rider of that pony may be lying injured in the cave-temple now. Anyway, we shall look there first. Come on."

Just as Rodmika had suggested, they found a long flight of crumbling stone stairs leading up the face of the hill to the stone gallery before the cave entrances. But inside they found no injured man. On the pitted stone floor was a smoldering fire, and near it, stretched out to dry, was a rabbit skin, neatly trimmed.

The older boy picked up a long, smooth iron-wood shaft that lay with one end in the ashes. "Whoever he is," he remarked, "has a very sharp knife, and he knows how to use it, too. See, he has made a spear and is hardening the point in the fire."

"Then let us get out of here before he returns," said Dobarra. "I'd rather be among wild animals than wild men."

"*Kabardar!*" exclaimed Rodmika in a low warning. He dropped the spear and pulled his younger brother to the floor. "That was an arrow."

"*What* was an arrow?" asked Dobarra staring wide-eyed at Rodmika.

"An arrow was shot into this chamber from the dense brush below the gallery. I heard it sing through the air and strike the ceiling. Go ahead of me. Crawl into the dark shadows behind the pillars along the wall—quickly."

Without another word they scrambled across the floor into the protective darkness. After a moment of watching and listening Dobarra spoke in a trembling voice, "I know what has brought us this ill luck."

147

"Luck!" scoffed Rodmika. "That word is used by those who are too lazy to find the real reason why things happen."

"Then I shall tell thee the real reason why this wild man has shot his arrow at us," returned Dobarra. "He wants his little silver thing that I found at the water's edge when we were looking for tracks."

"Why didst thou not tell me this before?" demanded Rodmika.

"I would have," explained Dobarra, "but the moment I picked it up the horse screamed, and I carried it clutched in my hand without thinking of it until now. Here, take it."

Rodmika took the small disk and moved his fingers over its uneven surface. "It's larger than an eight anna coin," he said, "but not so big as a rupee. I think it is a medal of some sort. Strike a light and we shall see what is inscribed upon it. But keep well behind this pillar, lest we be seen."

As the red glow of the burning thistledown shone on the small silver piece Rodmika leaned close and studied it. "It has on it a woman in flowing robes, bearing a shield in her hands," he said. "There is something strange about a wild man who uses bow and arrow, and wooden spear, yet possesses a silver medal and puts steel shoes upon his pony's hoofs. Now I see lettering upon the medal, and it is not our language."

Suddenly another arrow sang through the darkness, struck the ceiling and fell within arm's length of them. Rodmika recovered it. "The point has been cut from this one. It seems that the wild one does not want to injure us. Perhaps it is a warning. He wants us to leave his camp. Wait here a moment."

"Nay, brother, not alone in this darkness. I go with thee no matter what the danger."

"Then follow closely," said Rodmika. "I shall speak aloud in the language of the medal." Rodmika spoke in a loud voice as he neared the mouth of the cave. "We mean no harm to you. We wish to go in peace."

"Why, that was English!" exclaimed Dobarra in surprise.

149

"Yes," replied Rodmika, "the words upon the silver medal are in English."

They waited for an answer but none came. Presently the bushes that showed above the floor of the gallery began to move, and slowly a head rose above the ledge. The head was covered with tousled red hair, and through the hair peered two clear blue eyes. Between them was a turned-up nose in the middle of a round boyish face. Lips that were firm quickly lost their firmness and parted with a friendly grin.

Rodmika smiled and went forward to help the boy over the ledge, but Dobarra was too amazed to move. The boy's khaki shirt was bloodstained, and one arm was bandaged. There were torn places in his khaki shorts, and his sunburned knees showed the scratches of many thorns.

"How do you do?" greeted Rodmika. "You are an Englishman, aren't you?"

"I am an American," replied the boy, still grinning, "and I don't do very well, I suppose. I have been lost here for three days. I thought you fellows were wild men or something."

"That's what we thought you were," returned Rodmika, laughing. Then added, "We know some Americans who live at the Foundation beyond the jungle."

"That's where I live," said the boy. "You must know my grandfather, then. I am visiting him and my grandmother."

"I remember about you," said Rodmika. "Mr. Towers told me that you were coming. Is your name Towers, too?"

"Yes, my name is Towers. Call me Toppy. Everybody calls me Toppy."

"I am Rodmika," volunteered the Indian boy. "And my little brother's name is Dobarra. He doesn't speak very much English, yet, but he can understand most words."

Toppy extended his hand to the two boys and they timidly shook it. But when it was over, all three seemed to relax a little and speak more freely.

"A tiger jumped at my pony this morning," Toppy explained. "It was as big as the pony, and when its claws missed the pony's neck one raked my arm. The next thing I knew I was lying on the ground and the pony was kicking the tiger in the face and squealing like mad."

"Where is your pony now?" asked Rodmika.

"It ran away with the tiger after it."

Rodmika pointed to the bandage. "What about your arm?"

"It's nothing," said Toppy. "Not very deep. In a couple of days it will be all right. Say, I hope you can show me the way back to the Foundation."

"We will try," replied Rodmika. "That is why we are here. We are searching for a trail that will lead us there. But first we must take care of your wounded arm."

"It's nothing but a scratch," protested Toppy.

Rodmika's face clouded. "People who live in the jungle," he said solemnly, "learn that the scratch or bite of a wild animal often causes a man to get sick and die."

"Oh, I am too tough for that to happen to me," said Toppy with a laugh, but the laugh wasn't very hearty.

Rodmika turned to Dobarra and in their native dialect instructed him to build up the fire with dry sticks. Then back to

Toppy, he asked him to remove the bandage from the wound.

"It looks a little more inflamed," said the American when the bandage was off, "but I think it will heal all right."

"The doctor at the Foundation once told me how to treat such a wound," Rodmika explained, "but it will be painful."

Toppy's face became grave, and for a moment he said nothing. Then, "I don't know anything about the jungle, Rodmika. I'd be a sap not to have faith in what you say. What is the treatment?"

"We will have to burn deeply into the wound," said Rodmika, "with a piece of metal heated until it is a dull red."

"I remember, now," said Toppy. "That is called cauterizing." He reached into his pocket and drew out his knife. "Here, heat one of the blades. If it's got to be done, let's get it over with."

"Don't you have another piece of metal?" asked Rodmika. "So much heat will ruin a knife."

Toppy's hand went into his pocket again, but came out empty. "I had a quarter," he said, "but I must have lost it."

"This must be what you mean," said Rodmika, holding out the shiny silver disk. "Dobarra found it where the pavement comes out of the swamp. It is a very pretty medal."

"Medal?" said Toppy puzzled. "Just an American coin. See, it says 'United States of America—Quarter Dollar.'"

"We saw only the other side," explained Rodmika. "The side that has the motto that gave me courage to call you."

"In God We Trust," read Toppy, turning the coin over. "That's on almost all American coins. I never thought of it being a motto. But how will you hold the coin when it's red hot?"

"I'll wedge it into the split end of a piece of green bamboo," replied Rodmika.

As they watched the silver disk heat slowly, the Indian boys conversed in their native language, Rodmika explaining to his brother more fully what had happened to their new-found acquaintance.

"Then he must be very brave," observed Dobarra, giving Toppy an admiring glance. "Abdul has a scar where a leopard bit his shoulder, and Abdul is brave."

"There is no bravery in being bitten or scratched by a wild beast, little brother," said Rodmika, "no more bravery than in falling out of a tree. If our American friend is brave, we shall soon know it, for when the little medal begins to glow he must see it pressed into his wound, feel the searing pain, and smell his own flesh cooking."

"The medal is red now, Rodmika," advised Dobarra, closing his eyes and turning his head away. "I cannot look on while he suffers so."

"I am sorry we have no other medicines," said Rodmika turning to Toppy, "but the poison must be stopped now and this is the only thing that will stop it."

"I am beginning to think that you are right about the poison," admitted Toppy. "My whole arm feels feverish, and it is beginning to throb. Just give me something to hold onto and I can take it, no matter how much it hurts."

Rodmika handed him the iron-wood spear shaft. "Sit cross-legged near the fire," he directed, "place the shaft below your knees and grip it with both hands."

Toppy followed directions as Rodmika skillfully worked the coin into the split end of a bamboo arrow. Then without hesitation he pressed it into the inflamed wound and slowly drew it, hissing, from one end to the other.

Toppy's freckled face turned pale, and the color drained from his tight lips. Streams of sweat ran down his face, and his breath came in long hard sighs.

Against his will Dobarra found his eyes drawn toward the American boy's strained face, and big tears ran down his own brown cheeks. Only the steady Rodmika seemed unaffected— then it was over. Now Rodmika's hand began to tremble and cold perspiration stood out on his forehead. He put down the heated coin and breathed as though a heavy load had been lifted from his shoulders.

Toppy relaxed a little. His head bent forward, his chin touching his chest.

"Was I not right, Brother?" whispered Dobarra. "Our friend is truly brave."

Rodmika shook his head, then spoke to Dobarra. "Our work is not yet finished. The poison is gone, but the burned flesh must be treated so that it will heal. Climb into that tree beyond the gallery and strip the bark from those dead limbs. We will make tanbark tea to put on the wound."

When Dobarra returned, Rodmika had Toppy lying down with his head upon a pillow of leaves. "We will wait until tomorrow morning before we begin our search for the trail," Rodmika explained. "We all need the rest."

Toppy smiled. "You are thinking of me, Rodmika. But that's

all right. It was tough on you. I was watching your face. It hurt you as much as it did me. It takes a lot of bravery to stick a piece of red hot metal into a gash in a fellow's arm, and hear it sizzle."

"I think you ought to have a medal for bravery, and I am going to award you the side of that quarter with the motto on it."

OR THE SIXTH time that morning the three boys were stopped. Stopped by the reed-choked black waters of the great swamp. It was the great swamp all right, Rodmika was sure of that. During his years at the Foundation he had spent many days in the jungle along its edges. Often had he gone far out into the dark morass, but never had he found a way to cross it into the heart of Green Jungle. Now that he and Dobarra had crossed Green Jungle in the opposite direction, the great swamp was still the main obstacle that lay across the path between their home and the Foundation. But it had been crossed. Toppy had crossed it on his pony.

Rodmika turned away from the swamp and walked to where Toppy sat in the shade of a banyan tree testing the soreness of his wounded arm. "I think we've licked that poison for good," he said in a cheerful but tired voice. "If we could find where my pony brought me across the swamp, everything would be fine."

Rodmika was worried. "Tell me again, Toppy," he asked, "what was the swamp like where you crossed?"

"Well," answered the American boy, "I was so mixed up and lost that I didn't notice how it was. But I think it was very much like it is along here, with long finger-like ridges of rock extending out into the water. I rode the pony off the end of one of those ridges and tried to cross to another at one side, but when I got there I found just a rocky island. When I tried to get back I found myself on another rocky island just like it. After that I kept going through the tangle of vines, reeds, and mud from one island to the next. The farther I went, the denser the jungle became until it suddenly opened up and I rode out into the forest on this side. I don't know how many miles I came."

Rodmika was thoughtful for a moment. "Our only chance of getting back across," he said finally, "is to find that same chain of islands. But how to find it, when they all look alike at this end."

"Chup!" exclaimed Dobarra suddenly, silencing his brother. Until this moment he had been lying on the ground with his eyes closed. Now he sprang to his feet and stood in an alert crouch, his head turned to one side as he listened intently. "Didst thou hear it?" he asked Rodmika. " 'Twas so faint at first that I thought it was a dream, but when I opened my eyes I still heard it. The pony is screaming again, and it sounds far out in the great swamp."

A question was forming on Toppy's lips as he strove to follow Dobarra's native speech, but before he could ask it, it was answered for him by the shrill, faraway squeal of the pony.

"Ghora's alive," shouted Toppy, jumping to his feet. "The tiger is still after him, but he is still alive. Can we help him, Rodmika?"

"If we are fast enough, we can," said Rodmika over his

shoulder as he led off at a trot toward the sound. "He can help us too. I've heard that horses can always find their way home."

"That's right," said Toppy. "On my father's ranch at home the horses sometimes find their way back when they have been sold to other ranches over a hundred miles away."

"What about the tiger?" asked Dobarra uneasily. "Will we use Toppy's bow and arrows or thy sheath knife?"

Rodmika laughed and translated his question to Toppy, then added, "I don't think it is the tiger. I am sure he got away from the tiger soon after he was attacked. It may be crocodiles this time."

Their progress was slow in spite of the fact that they kept at a tiring trot most of the time. As they came to each low ridge that led out into the swamp, Rodmika stopped to search for signs of the pony's passage. At last he was rewarded. The tracks were easy to see and led from island to island into the swamp.

Feeling their way before them with long sticks, they waded into the dark water. It grew deeper with each step and slimy water weeds pulled at their legs. For a long time they heard no sounds beyond them and hoped that the pony had again escaped its attacker.

"Watch carefully for crocodiles," warned Rodmika. "They won't usually charge a human being; but if one of them has drawn blood from the pony there will be a number of them about, and they will be excited enough to go after anything that moves."

They were halfway between two islands when Rodmika stopped. Moving cautiously from side to side he studied the jungle ahead of him. "What color was your pony, Toppy?" he asked in a low voice.

"Gray, almost white. Why? Do you see him?"

"No," replied Rodmika, "I see something black moving about on that island. I have an idea what it is, but I'm not sure. Make no noise and as soon as we reach the island we'll climb a tree."

They had hardly got into a safe position in the tree when Toppy whispered excitedly, "It's a bear. A black bear with a hump on its back."

"I thought so," said Rodmika from higher up. "I don't see the bear, but I do see the pony. He is standing in a clump of bamboo. He seems all right."

"Will the bear try to eat him?" asked Toppy.

"No. Bhalu is a sloth bear. He usually eats nothing but fruit, honey, insects, and things like that; but he is angry at the pony for some reason. When Bhalu is angry he may attack anything."

For a while the grunting and growling bear was lost from sight, but Rodmika could tell something of its movements by watching the head and ears of the pony. Presently Ghora stamped a steel-shod hoof and nervously began jerking his chin back against his slick gray neck. The bear was advancing toward him, grunting and snarling savagely.

Ghora screamed again, but more in anger than in fear. With a flash of wavy mane he whirled about and lashed out furiously with both back feet.

The boys in the tree heard the steel shoes strike solidly three times in rapid succession. Then to the scream of the pony was added the howl of the bear.

"Bhalu is hurt," shouted Rodmika. "And when he is hurt badly he cries and runs away. Here he comes."

As he spoke a large ball of black fur rolled from the bamboo clump, bellowing as though ten tigers were after it. One of the bear's forefeet seemed to drag, but it lost no time in making good use of the other three. Still bawling, it made straight for the tree which held the three boys, dashed past it and plunged into the swamp. Churning water to foam it reached the island behind them and kept going.

Toppy gave a low whistle of relief and looked at Rodmika. "Did you know that the bear was not going to climb this tree?"

"Yes," returned Rodmika, grinning, "these bears are not good climbers even when they have four good legs."

"I wish I'd known that," said Toppy, "it would have saved me a bad half minute. But, say, that wasn't the same bear I saw at first. The other one had a big hump on his back."

"Are you sure about that hump?" asked Rodmika, turning toward the howling bear to make sure that it was in full retreat before leading the way to the ground.

"I saw it as plain as day," Toppy insisted. "It had a thick hump right over its shoulders, and the one that ran away didn't have one."

"That's fine," said Rodmika, dropping to the ground; "now we'll see if we can find the other bear."

"You are not trying to joke with me, are you?" demanded Toppy, remaining where he was. "Or maybe you think I am joking with you."

"No," replied Rodmika with a delighted gleam in his dark eyes, "I am sure there is another bear on this island."

To their ears came a faint squeal, and Dobarra tumbled out of the tree with shouts of *"Bhalu batcha log, Bhalu batcha log!"*

"What is he saying?" asked Toppy, more puzzled than ever.

Rodmika laughed. "Exactly he says, 'Bears brother people.' He means little bears. Abdul the hunter taught him that expression. Little bears travel on their mother's back when they are young and helpless. She must have hidden them in the grass before she attacked the pony."

When Toppy and Rodmika reached the squealing cubs they found Dobarra pulling them from a crevice in the rocks. They were two sprawling creatures no bigger than kittens, and as black as crows, except for a snow-white spot at the base of their throats.

Rodmika knelt to examine them. "They have just got their eyes open," he announced. "They will make clever pets until they get too big to play with. We will take them with us. I don't think their mother will come back for them."

Toppy reached down, rubbed their heads with one finger, then turned away to attend to his pony.

Dobarra touched his brother's arm. "Hast thou forgot the young pig I captured?"

"I remember," replied Rodmika, "but in this case we have no choice. And besides they have already stopped their crying. The beasts of the jungle will not come out here on these islands. If they become aroused at Bhalu's howling they will follow her."

"Boy, is this pony glad to see me!" said Toppy, leading Ghora from the thicket. "The reins are broken off, and the saddle blanket is gone, but the saddle is here hanging under him."

"Did the tiger hurt him?" asked Rodmika.

"There are two long gashes in his shoulder," replied Toppy, "but they don't seem very deep. The saddle must have saved him. The leather is ripped and cut in several places."

162

"We can make reins from vines," suggested Rodmika, "so that you can ride."

"That's a good idea," said Toppy, "but I won't need to ride. We'll put Dobarra in the saddle with the bear cubs. He looks pretty tired."

When Rodmika had made it clear to his little brother that he was to ride the pony and hold the two baby bears in the folds of his *dhoti* Dobarra looked shyly from Toppy to Ghora and back to Toppy. Then, smiling broadly, he spoke in hesitant English, "I thank you, Toppy, very little."

Both the older boys laughed. "Very *much*," corrected Rodmika, "not very *little*."

"He'll get along," said Toppy, dropping a hand upon Dobarra's shoulder. "I wish I had the courage to try using your language."

Although with Dobarra riding they went much faster, their progress was still slow through the wet slippery jungle. It was dark and they were nearly exhausted when they reached the hill on the edge of the swamp. A light flickered in the forest ahead of them. Rodmika cupped his hands about his mouth and sang out in a high-pitched "Coo-ee-ee" that carried well through the trees.

Mingled with the echoes that followed came the report of a rifle and much shouting. As they continued their march toward the light they realized that the light was coming to meet them. Presently they could see several men on horseback.

"It's your grandfather, Toppy," said Rodmika. "It's Mr. Towers."

After that there was much calling back and forth until the two parties were together.

"We had about worn ourselves out trying to find you, young man," said Mr. Towers, giving Toppy a hearty hug. "We were returning home after a two-day search of the swamp. The station wagon has been sent to Kumba to bring a tracker from the forest guards. Say, what's wrong with your arm?"

"It's just a burn now," replied Toppy, excited in spite of his weariness. "I'll tell you about it later. You know my two guides, I think, Rodmika and Dobarra."

"I should say I do. But, wait. How did you boys get on this side of Green Jungle?"

"We crossed it," answered Rodmika.

"You crossed from the Kumba side?" The speaker was a tall young man who stepped into the light. "You two boys alone. Why, how could you? It's twenty miles of water."

Mr. Towers placed a hand on the young man's shoulder. "Let's get these boys home. I imagine they have more to tell than we have time to hear out in this dark jungle." Then turning to Rodmika, "Shake hands with Jim Lawrence, the new surveyor. Jim, this is Rodmika, the boy I said could tell you more about Green Jungle than all your maps."

"And this is my little brother, Dobarra," said Rodmika, waving toward the pony.

"Not only Dobarra," added Toppy, "but a couple of Bhalu's children as well." At a word from Rodmika, Dobarra proudly held up the squirming cubs.

"Well, what do you think of that!" said Mr. Towers in high

good humor. "If this isn't something to write home about. We get out and beat up the jungle for two days, half expecting to find that bears had gotten this grandson of mine, and here he comes in with two new friends and a couple of bears to boot."

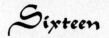

THE ARRIVAL OF the little party at the Foundation Buildings caused a stir of frantic activity. Although it was past nine o'clock Fernando, the cook, came running from his bungalow, shouting to Dussi, the *hamal,* to get a charcoal fire going in the kitchen.

Mrs. Towers suppressed her relief and happiness at having her grandson safely out of the jungle and quietly gave instructions. "Dussi, see that there is plenty of hot water. They will want showers before they eat. And, Fernando, warm those two roast chickens. With hot pulse and marrow, some fresh fruit and cold milk they should last until morning."

Then as the men and boys ate, she hovered over them. The boys ate in tired silence, but the two men talked to her relaying all that Rodmika and Toppy had told them.

When they had finished, Mrs. Towers said, more to Mr. Towers and Jim Lawrence than to the boys, "Don't start talking tonight. You all need rest. So off to bed with you."

"But the bears," protested Toppy. "They haven't had a thing to eat since we got them."

"I'll get Fernando to give them a bowl of milk. You boys are dead on your feet. Rodmika, you and Dobarra take the room next to Toppy's."

"Now, wait a minute, Lena," said Mr. Towers. "In my twenty-five years out here I've learned something about the Indian sloth bear and a little about their cubs. They have to be taught to eat and it isn't so easy. I knew of a pair once that starved before they learned."

"Maybe Rodmika knows how to feed them," suggested Toppy.

"I have taught motherless calves to eat," said Rodmika, "and once I taught a baby mongoose to lap milk. I have never tried to teach baby bears to eat."

They went into the kitchen where Fernando had fitted out a basket for the two small bears to lie in. When the lid was lifted the little creatures, left off sucking the pads of their paws, raised their heads and began squealing hungrily.

Mr. Towers handed a bowl of milk to Rodmika. "You might try the mongoose treatment first."

Rodmika dipped a finger into the milk and touched it to the nose of one of the cubs. The cub ignored it. Then the boy dipped his little finger well into the milk and thrust it into the bear's tiny mouth. The little animal sucked vigorously. Rodmika repeated this a half dozen times for each cub.

"It will take forever to feed them that way," said Toppy.

"Try this," said Mrs. Towers coming into the kitchen. She handed Rodmika a medicine dropper with a hole punched in the end of the rubber bulb. Rodmika filled it with milk and put the bulb into the cub's mouth. It chewed and sucked but all could see that no milk was leaving the medicine dropper.

Dobarra timidly whispered into his brother's ear. Rodmika laughed. "He says that since bears suck their paws why not put the paws into the milk."

"Good boy, Dobarra," said Toppy. "Give it a try, Rodmika."

Rodmika tried it and it worked. They all laughed in delight as the little creatures licked and sucked at their wet paws. Finally Mr. Towers said, "That's still not the solution. We can't spend our time dipping bear paws in milk. Let me try something." Lifting a cub by the loose skin at the back of its neck he moved it to the edge of the bowl and pushed its muzzle into the white liquid. The cub coughed and sneezed and licked its lips, then began to lap. "That does it," said Mr. Towers, reaching for the second cub. It took three duckings in the milk to start it lapping, but once it began they made short work of the entire contents of the small bowl.

"That will be enough for tonight," said Mr. Towers.

"How often will they have to be fed?" asked Toppy.

"Every two hours in the daytime for the next week or so. Then we will add honey, and later some cooked oatmeal. Soon they will be eating all kinds of fruit as well."

They placed the cubs back in the basket where they curled up together, noisily sucking the pads of their paws until they fell asleep.

Mr. Towers followed Toppy to his room to examine his wounded arm, while the two Indian boys went to their room next door. Dobarra was asleep as soon as he was in bed, but Rodmika was too excited even to close his eyes. It was difficult to realize that he had crossed Green Jungle. He could hardly wait until tomorrow to tell the surveyor of the many miles of high ground he had found there.

The door across from the bed creaked slowly open and the shadowy form of a man was in the room. "Rodmika," said Mr. Towers quietly.

"Yes, Sir," answered the boy.

"How does it feel to be back at the Foundation?"

"Very good, Sir. And now that we have found a way to cross Green Jungle could the surveyor *sahib* teach me high school subjects?"

"I think it could be arranged," answered Mr. Towers. The door creaked once more, but before it closed he spoke again. "You did a pretty good doctoring job on Toppy's arm. In fact you probably saved his life. I don't think Toppy will soon forget it either."

* * *

The next day the boys lay about the shady compound resting and taking turns at feeding the cubs. Jim Lawrence came in from the fields at eleven and sat back in a long-armed chair on the veranda, smoking his pipe. He watched the boys for a while then called to Rodmika. "I wish you'd tell me something about what you found in Green Jungle."

"Do you mean, Sir, the old highway?" answered Rodmika.

The surveyor dropped his feet to the floor and sat upright. "Highway!"

"Highway!" repeated Mrs. Towers coming out onto the veranda. "Don't tell me you found a highway in Green Jungle."

"It is very old," said Rodmika.

169

"But it's still good in places," added Toppy. "I rode Ghora over part of it."

"Except for places where it is under water or beneath the soil of the jungle," said Rodmika, "a bullock cart could be driven over it for nearly ten miles. Then there are three or four miles through the grasslands where a new road could be built easily."

Jim Lawrence jumped to his feet. "Let me get my map," he said, going into the house.

Mrs. Towers smiled and shook her head. "A surveyor can't talk without a map. Rodmika, can you read one?"

M·A

"I just know what you taught us about maps in geography."

"I am afraid that wasn't much," said Mrs. Towers, "but it may help you tell Jim what he wants to know."

At that moment the young surveyor came back onto the veranda holding a pencil in his mouth and unfolding a map about a yard square. He knelt and spread it on the smooth stone floor.

"Now," said Lawrence, pointing to the map with his pencil, "we are here where it says 'Valdapur.' That is the village here at the Foundation. And there to the East of the Foundation is Green Jungle. See, it says, 'Unadministered territory.' That means Green Jungle cannot be penetrated except at great effort. The government hasn't considered it worth the effort and cost to survey it. The way the whole area is shaded indicates that it is under water."

"But it's not," said Toppy. "There is at least one hill in there. The cave where I camped was in a hill."

"And another hill where the old highway crosses the lake from the grassland to the forest," added Rodmika.

"Can you point out on the map where the highway goes?" Jim Lawrence asked Rodmika.

Rodmika took the pencil and studied the map. "I see Kumba village," he said, "but where is my father's farm?"

"Do you find a place labeled 'ruins'?" asked Mrs. Towers. "It is in old English letters near the edge of the jungle on the eastern side."

"Yes, here it is," said Lawrence.

"Well," Mrs. Towers continued, "Mr. Towers told me years

ago that those ruins were the stone walls of Jankari's father's house."

Rodmika touched the place with the pencil point and drew a line northwestward into the jungle. "For a day and a half I followed the course of the birds in this direction to the grasslands."

"How many miles from your home to the grasslands?" asked the surveyor, taking a pair of dividers from his pocket and beginning to measure along the line Rodmika had drawn.

"A mile and a half from our house to the edge of the jungle, and about seven, I think, through the jungle to the grasslands."

With a red pencil Jim Lawrence made a mark on Rodmika's line. "Then the grassland begins here. Now how far across, and in what direction?"

"Almost north, but still a little west," the boy explained, "was the hill where the old highway leaned on its side like a wall. It is about three miles across the grasslands to the hill."

The surveyor drew lines as Rodmika talked. "I followed the highway straight northward for two miles through the forest to the old palace."

"Palace!" Mrs. Towers, Jim Lawrence, and Toppy exclaimed in unison.

"You didn't tell me about a palace," said Toppy.

Rodmika grinned. "So many things were happening I didn't think about it. My brother and I spent the monsoon there raising a crop of rice in the old courtyard."

"Can you tie that!" said the surveyor. "And the whole world going by a map that says the entire area is under water."

"Here comes the station wagon with the tracker from Kumba," said Mrs. Towers, getting up from her chair. "Too bad he's had that long trip for nothing."

Mr. Towers rode up to the compound gate at that moment, dismounted and handed his reins over to Garba, the old Hindu *syce* who had been waiting there with a handful of carrots for the pony. "Here comes the station wagon, Lena," he called to his wife. "It's loaded down with trackers, I suppose. Rodmika, how would you and Dobarra like to go back to Kumba in the station wagon. The trip that took you a week by bullock cart can be made in seven hours by car."

The station wagon rumbled over the crest of the hill at the edge of the forest and coasted down the rain-washed road to the compound. As it rolled to a stop the boys joined Mr. Towers at the gate.

A blue-turbaned head with the brass number "29" pinned to it popped out of the window beside the driver. The face beneath it wore a contemptuous frown and was adorned with a gray mustache the ends of which the owner's fingers were nervously tugging. "Aye," he said in the vernacular, "thou wert right, Master. There stands the jungle boy before our very eyes. And he has, no doubt, found the lost one. *Salaam*, thou," he added with a wave to Rodmika.

"*Salaam*," returned Rodmika. Then to Toppy he explained, "That is Guga Dall, the forest guard. And look, there inside, my teacher, Vallabiah. He is smiling as if he were greatly pleased about something."

Jim Lawrence came out to the station wagon and stood beside

Mr. Towers as Guga Dall and Vallabiah alighted. There was much *salaaming* as greetings were exchanged; then they all shook hands western style. After that Mr. Towers was lavish in his praise of Vallabiah whom he had known many years before.

"My first agricultural pamphlet was translated into both *Hindi* and *Urdu* by this gentleman," Mr. Towers declared. "And to this day there hasn't been a better translation of anything we've published. And not only is he a master of languages, Lawrence, but a fine teacher as well. Jankari's boy, young Rodmika, is a student of his."

Old Vallabiah laughed delightedly. "I taught him nothing about the jungle. And I daresay it was he who found the American lad and brought him out of the swamp."

Compliments were then showered down upon Rodmika, and he was glad when Vallabiah broke it off with a statement to Mr. Towers. "I hope you will forgive me for begging a ride in your motorcar, Sir, but I have been appointed magistrate of the Kumba district, and I have received instructions from the Department of Public Works urging that I confer with you and Mr. Lawrence upon the matter of the bridge at Wardlo ferry."

"You are welcome to a ride in one of our cars at any time and for any reason, Sir," answered Mr. Towers. "And about the Wardlo bridge we are especially anxious to cooperate with the Public Works Department."

"Upon that score," said Vallabiah, "I am afraid that I have bad news for you. It is true that such a bridge would save some sixty miles of the journey from here to Kumba, but the PWD engineers tell me that in view of the five miles of earthen embankment necessary in addition to the three-hundred-foot steel bridge, the money for this most desirable bit of construction will not be forthcoming. Our new government is hard pressed for funds with which to buy such things as steel and concrete. What is spent for road construction for the next few years must be limited, in our case, at least, to labor and the use of such materials as abound locally."

Rodmika's eyes shifted quickly from one face to the other of the men as they talked. Disappointment showed in deep lines upon Mr. Towers' face. He seemed to grow older with every discouraging word that Vallabiah spoke, while at the same time the smile that gleamed from the half-hidden eyes beneath Vallabiah's great overshadowing red turban became more pronounced. Jim Lawrence's expression of disappointment slowly gave way to an amused grin that showed his strong white teeth.

"May I ask you a question, Sir?" he asked the bearded old Hindu pundit.

"You may," answered Vallabiah.

"Then I would like for you to tell us, if by any chance, *you* suggested to the PWD engineers that the Wardlo bridge project be abandoned."

"I must confess that I did," said Vallabiah. "Information recently given me in Kumba indicates the Wardlo bridge cutoff would be entirely impractical."

Mr. Towers' mouth fell open and he gasped. "After all the work we've done on that. Why the Foundation has spent thousands of rupees to get that project through. They don't realize how much benefit it would be to this district to bring Valdapur and Kumba closer together."

Lawrence's grin grew broader. "I have another question," he said quickly. "If the person responsible for your decision to advise the government against the Wardlo bridge is here will you please point him out?"

"Impossible!" snorted Mr. Towers.

Old Vallabiah chuckled deeply through his white beard. "He is here and I shall gladly point him out." One long finger came up and swung about to come to rest pointing at Rodmika. "This young man has wrecked the plans of the best engineers in the country, as well as the best the American Foundation has."

"What's going on here?" shouted Mr. Towers. "Why am I in the dark about all this? We don't get a road that will save sixty miles from here to Kumba and you are all happy about it."

Jim Lawrence and old Vallabiah laughed heartily, and Rodmika, not knowing exactly what was going on, grinned uneasily.

"It's something to be happy about," said Lawrence. "We don't get the road that will save sixty miles, but unless I miss my guess we are going to get one that will save considerably more than one hundred miles."

"Exactly," said Vallabiah. "When young Rodmika visited his parents in the middle of the monsoon he told them what he had found in the jungle. Many miles of high dry land, and in some places a ready-paved highway."

"That boy, that boy," said Mr. Towers. "You know, when he left here with his mother and the small children he said that he was determined to find a way to cross Green Jungle. It sounded like a child's dream."

Jim Lawrence was unfolding his map again, but Mr. Towers stopped him. "You can just put that away until after tiffin," he said. "These people have come a long way. When we've all had a good meal and some rest we can get back to this map business."

* * *

After the heavy Indian tiffin the men rested on the veranda and talked while the boys huddled about the basket containing the bears. Soon Guga Dall arrived from Valdapur village where he had eaten with a cousin who kept a tobacco shop in the bazaar. He grinned down at the small creatures. *"Bhalu batcha log,"* he said softly. "I have seen many such as these in my lifetime in the forest." He hesitated while Rodmika translated into English what he said. "I remember one camp in the reserved forest of Nur when I was but a young man. A great she-bear killed a woodcutter, and my *sahib* took his double-barreled rifle and tracked her to a cave in a bushy hillside.

"Alas, she would not come out. Bears will stay forever in a hole. They are not like the great cats of the jungle. A tiger will go into a hole, but it will not stay. Neither the tiger nor the leopard likes small places. The bear will stay forever." The forest guard laughed and pulled at his gray mustache as he spoke.

"My *sahib* was very angry. 'We will dig out the bear,' he said. He sent for bars, and drills and mallets, and more men. There was a hullabaloo as we dug, and at night we kept a big fire

177

going. My *sahib* stood ready all the time with his double-barreled rifle. For two days we broke the rocks and dug them out. Then at last we saw something white in the dark hole. It was white and shaped like the wide horseshoe. To my *sahib* I said, 'It is the white collar on Bhalu's neck, the white horseshoe collar that all our jungle bears wear. Shoot that, *sahib,* and the killer of the woodcutter will surely die.' Boom. My *sahib* shot.

"After the echoes there was silence. Bhalu was dead. Then we heard cries of the little ones, and when we dragged Bhalu out, two such as these clung to the hair of her shoulders. My *sahib* put them in his coat pocket. For three months thereafter I was mother to two small bears. *Sahibs* have strange ideas. All his anger for the old bear turned into love for the young ones.

" '*Sahib,*' I said, 'lest these creatures grow up to kill other woodcutters, let them die now.' 'For shame, Guga Dall,' he said, 'wouldst thou kill innocent babes?' Ugh! Who teaches them in their land across the seas? Who teaches the white *sahib* to be so strange?" He smiled and gestured toward Toppy, then to Rodmika. "Keep him in India so that he will grow up to be reasonable."

Rodmika translated this also, and they all laughed. Toppy promised that he would try to learn enough while he was in India to grow up to be reasonable.

"Rodmika!" called a voice from the veranda. All heads grouped about the bears' basket turned.

"There . . . see," said Guga Dall in a whisper. Both Jim Lawrence and Vallabiah were motioning to Rodmika to come. "The young *sahib* on the veranda is not reasonable," said the forest guard. "He asks the impossible. He curls his fingers *upward,* which say 'Come to me, fly through the air.' Now see the bearded one he curls his fingers *downward,* which say, 'Come to me, walk on the ground.'"

As Rodmika rose to go to the veranda, Guga Dall chuckled and added, "Behold, the jungle boy obeys the Hindu, who is reasonable. He walks on the ground."

* * *

Most of the afternoon was spent on the map, but as the sun was lowering into the haze over Green Jungle, Vallabiah drew Rodmika aside and they walked away from the compound into the forest.

"The road is now assured," said the old man. "Last year in your father's bullock cart it was nine days from the Foundation to your new home. Tomorrow in the motorcar it will be but nine hours. Next year, through Green Jungle it will be less than nine hours on foot, and in a motorcar only a half hour."

"That will be wonderful," said Rodmika. "But I shall have no motorcar."

"You have forgotten Hassin, the bus driver," said Vallabiah. "Already his uncle, who owns three busses, is negotiating for another to be run daily and return from Kumba to Valdapur and beyond."

"Then we can go to the Foundation to school," said Rodmika in wonder. For a few minutes he was silent; then he spoke again with worry in his voice. "What will happen to the animals? What will happen to Gonda, the great bull elephant, and the wild buffaloes? They need deep, faraway jungles. Men with guns might go where busses will take them. Hunters, not like Abdul, who kills only those that disturb the jungle, will go there and kill for pleasure."

"I have spoken to the Prime Minister's secretary about that," said the old man. "I think all of Green Jungle will become not only a reserved forest, but a refuge for all animals.

"Now, I have something to ask thee, little brother." For greater intimacy Vallabiah spoke in their native dialect.

"Ask, O Father."

"Thou hast said little about the old palace, and nothing about the sign of the cobra crown upon thy chest. Still, I know that thou didst find the sign."

"The wagging tongue of my brother," said Rodmika, "the little monkey. He exaggerates greatly sometimes. He is young and things grow in his mind with telling about them." Rodmika would not mislead his old friend, but he hoped that he wouldn't be questioned too closely. He remembered the feeling that had come over him in the dungeon. It began when Dobarra had found the golden links hanging from under the lid of the closed copper chest. The links with the golden image of the cobra crown at the end of it. In a way it seemed to prepare him for the finding of the copper medallion showing the ancient king and his young prince, both having the sign of the cobra upon their chests and wearing cobra crowns upon their heads.

Dobarra hadn't seen the medallion, so he couldn't tell about it. And where Rodmika had hidden it he was sure it would never be found. The road would bring many people to the old palace. They would see all the old things in the dungeon, but his secret would be safe.

Vallabiah drew a purse from his sash, opened it and took out a small object wrapped in paper. "Hast thou seen this before?" he asked, opening the paper to reveal the small image of the seven-headed cobra.

Rodmika gasped. "Dobarra cut it loose."

"Yes, with a copper spearhead. He brought it to thy father as a gift. It was that evidence that turned the affair of the road in our favor. The Prime Minister's secretary was much impressed. The historical society will send a man to go with the PWD engineer and Mr. Lawrence when thou leadest them to the palace."

"What of our rice field in the courtyard?" asked Rodmika. "Will we be permitted to plant there again?"

"Who has a better right than the successor to that ancient throne?" The old man's smile gleamed for a moment. Then his face became solemn. He scratched thoughtfully in his white beard and gazed through the branches above and for a moment watched a scissor-tailed drongo dart upward into the waning sunlight to catch an invisible insect. "If we could only find some proof, real proof that I could lay before His Excellency. I thought thou might have found something. We may find something yet. The study of ancient peoples has been fascinating to me, and to achieve some success in that field would be most pleasing in my old age. To link the past with the present in some positive form is a worthy goal for a scholar. I am afraid I have failed."

Rodmika lowered his eyes from his old teacher's face and looked unseeing at his bare feet. "O Father," he said after a moment of silence. "I have found what thou seekest. I have found it hammered in thin copper. Then I hid it where even I may not recover it."

Vallabiah lifted his hands to the boy's shoulders. "That I seemed, somehow, to know, my son. In thine eyes I seemed to see a haunting pride. At first I took it to mean a bragging vanity aroused by all the praise the *sahibs* gave thee at bringing the American lad safely out of the swamp. But no, that was no feat for one born of the jungle, it was something deeper, something new in the young pupil I thought I knew so well. What is this thing that holds thee entranced as though thou wert a peacock preening itself before a mirror?"

Rodmika could not lift his head. "On the copper medallion was a king and his court," said the boy. "Beside the king upon the same dais sat a child prince. Upon their heads alone rested the cobra crown, and upon their chests alone was the sign of the seven-headed cobra, exact in every way with the one which my father placed upon me.

" 'Go into the jungle and seek thyself,' was thy command, O wise one. I sought and I found. At first I felt fear, then I was proud, for after my father I was king of Hara Daldal.

"I wanted no one else to know of it. This is no day for kings. People would point and say, 'Look, the jungle boy who calls himself king—king of monkeys, serpents, and screaming birds.' Instead I would keep it a secret. Then no one would laugh and no one could take it from me. I alone would know the truth and the truth would warm me and I could say silently, 'I am king of Hara Daldal.' "

"And now, little brother?"

"And now, O Father, I am ashamed. And when I am at home again I will bow before my father and say that I am ashamed. If there is a rightful heir to this kingdom which has been over a thousand years dead, it is he, and not I. For thee, O wise one, I will find the copper thing."

The brief jungle twilight had settled over the forest. A jungle cock called from its roost. The boy and the old man turned back toward the Foundation. "There will, no doubt, be a number of fertile spots in such a great jungle," observed Vallabiah. "Our new government will want the best use possible made of it. I should think that an intelligent young farmer who could prove his ability to produce good crops might be given a chance to farm a portion of that new land on most agreeable terms."

Rodmika felt that a great weight had been lifted from his shoulders. The cobra crown and the rich robes he had so often worn in his dreams seemed to slip to the floor of the jungle. Once more the damp smell of the earth reminded him of the black soil of the courtyard at Kala tank, and a swift pain of uneasiness swept through him as he thought of his unprotected field with the heavy grain heads ripening in the sun. "Will I be at home by this hour tomorrow?" he asked.

"Long before," replied the old man, "if the motorcar leaves here at dawn."

"Then on the next morning we can start back to our field at the old palace, my brother and I. We shouldn't have left it for so long, but still it is a good thing we did, for Toppy might not have found his way home alone."

The old man chuckled. "The things we do are all mixed together, good and bad, wise and unwise, like grain on the threshing floor. As it is being trampled under the feet of bullocks or ponies it seems a hopeless mess. Then in a light breeze it is winnowed, the chaff blows away, and we see the clean brown grain fill bag after bag. It gives us courage and wisdom to face the next season, confident that we can separate the good from the bad with a more skillful hand."

They walked on, listening to the evening sounds of the jungle. Two spotted owlets quarreled in a wild fig tree, and a browsing *cheetal* barked from the vale below. Gradually a jingle of bronze bells came to them from the trail along the hillside above. The sound grew louder as the bells came nearer. Rodmika laughed softly. "It is Swanji, the Dak-runner, and he is running with all speed, although he is still a mile from the Foundation. He must have an important letter for someone."